Praise for *The Paper Bridge* – Expa

This personal portrait is more than a trav
travel - time travel – [and] its astute obse
of history. *Daily Mail*

. . . informative and evocative . . . a poignant story of burning as well as
building bridges. *Independent on Sunday*

Of all the books timed to coincide with the twentieth anniversary of the
revolutions of 1989, The Paper Bridge may have the most charm.

Victor Sebestyen, *Mail on Sunday*

. . . what comes through is a more complex picture than is often given in
accounts of 'life behind the Iron Curtain', where everything is seen in strict
black-and-white terms, with hardly any shading . . . certainly an enjoyable
read. *Budapest Times*

Praise for *The Paper Bridge* – Original 1981 edition

[Monica Porter's] book is jolly and wistful – and rather passionate...She
examines her own place both inside and outside Hungary movingly... "As it
happens, Hungary is not a difficult country to love," she writes. Indeed it is
not, and Monica Porter's book shows that admirably.

William Shawcross, *The Spectator*

. . . Charming, unaffected...A sincere, essentially saddening book – but
cheerfulness keeps breaking in. *Sunday Telegraph*

[Monica Porter's] rediscovery of her country and relatives, and her thoughts
about the present state of Hungary are never less than interesting, and often
have an insight denied to political theorists. *The Good Book Guide*

. . . a fascinating account of life in modern-day Hungary...which will appeal
both to migrants – from any country – and to Australians interested in
understanding the double life which so many fellow citizens can never
completely escape. *The Australian*

In this quiet, simply written, affecting book, [Monica Porter] describes the
roots-seeking journey she and her four-year-old son made to Budapest 25
years after the abortive revolt . . . Porter comes to understand her native
land's tragic past and "stagnating" present . . . She has built a delicate bridge
between the past and her chosen way of life in London.

Publishers Weekly

The author has a sharp eye, a warm heart and an insight belying her years.

Francis Rentoul, BBC World Service

LONG LOST

The Story of the Newspaper Column
that Started the Reunion Industry

MONICA PORTER

QUARTET BOOKS

First published in 2010 by
Quartet Books Limited
A member of the Namara Group
27 Goodge Street, London WIT 2LD

A catalogue record for this book
is available from the British Library

ISBN   978 0 7043 7201 6

Typeset by Antony Gray
Printed and bound in Great Britain by
T J International Ltd, Padstow, Cornwall

Contents

Acknowledgements

I am indebted to the *Daily Mail*, especially to Editor Paul Dacre, for turning the Missing and Found column into what can now reasonably be called an institution and for making it my baby.

My supervising editor on the paper, Andy Simpson – a veritable walking encyclopaedia and something of a *Daily Mail* institution himself – has been unfailingly supportive to me throughout the years. I am most grateful for that.

Gill Whitley, who together with her husband John was the column's initial inspiration and who remains its behind-the-scenes researcher, is admirably devoted to her 'people-finding' mission. I salute her.

But most of all I want to thank the many thousands of ordinary, decent people who have written to me over the past eleven years and entrusted me with their personal, often deeply touching stories – whether or not those stories have appeared in Missing and Found. They are the people to whom this book is most warmly and wholeheartedly dedicated.

CHAPTER ONE

How It All Began

One day in early 1998 the larger-than-life Fleet Street editor Sir David English, then Editor-in-Chief of Associated Newspapers, was going through the pile of letters on his desk when one item in particular roused his interest. It was from a *Daily Mail* reader (the *Mail*, of course, being the flagship title in the Associated stable) who wished to inform Sir David of a recent happy episode in his life.

The reader, who lived in Somerset, explained that due to a family break-up many years earlier his wife had lost touch with her much-loved brother. She was getting old and had yearned to find him again before it was too late, but had no idea where or how to look for him. Now, to their great delight, his wife and her brother had been reunited. And they had a stranger to thank – a woman called Gill Whitley, who lived up north in Anglesey.

Gill had previously managed, against the odds, to track down her husband John's mother, whom he hadn't seen for decades, which led to an emotional and joyful reunion between mother and son. That success had spurred her on to help others reconnect with their estranged relatives and friends, and among those she helped was the wife of the letter-writer from Somerset. She didn't do this for profit; it wasn't a business. It was more of a mission. Gill provided her voluntary service – which she named Searching for a Memory – purely for the satisfaction of doing something worthwhile that could change people's lives, the way John's life had been changed by finding his mother.

The Somerset man had been deeply impressed by the way Gill had brought about his wife and brother-in-law's reunion, and the purpose of his letter to Sir David was to suggest that the *Daily Mail* might wish to publish an article about Gill and what she was doing. After all, it was a classic feel-good story.

The Editor-in-Chief hadn't reached his exalted status among the Fleet Street greats without a keen instinct for what his readers wanted, and he recognised at once that this was indeed a human-interest story which would appeal to the *Daily Mail*'s broad, middle-class, middle-brow constituency. He passed the letter on to the paper's features department, with a memo instructing that it be followed up. It would make a good feature article, he advised, perhaps even a series of some kind. The paper duly contacted Gill to set the ball rolling.

Now, when it comes to the news, newspapers move like lightning – apart from anything else, they need to beat (or at least keep up with) their rivals. But in the realm of non-time-sensitive feature ideas, there is often a back-burner mentality. So while there was definite interest in Gill's 'people-finding' service (and the fact that the story idea had been put forward by David English himself made it all the more imperative), the ball nevertheless rolled slowly.

In June of that year Associated Newspapers suffered a major blow with sixty-seven-year-old Sir David's death from a stroke. He had been with the company for almost thirty years, originally as Editor of the *Daily Sketch*, and was responsible for transforming the *Daily Mail* into a journalistic powerhouse during his tenure as its Editor from 1971 to 1992. Soon after his death, Paul Dacre – not far behind English in the legendary-editor stakes –

took over as Associated's Editor-in-Chief, as well as retaining his position as Editor of the *Mail*.

In due course Dacre turned his attention to the Gill Whitley matter, and made a decision. The theme of reconnecting long lost friends and family members, he felt, would strike a chord with the paper's readership. Most people have someone in their life with whom they lost touch and would like to be reunited. And a newspaper such as the *Mail*, with millions of readers in Britain and many abroad, could provide the perfect vehicle for making that happen. The Editor decided to make space for a regular weekly slot featuring the stories of those who are searching for the 'someone' missing from their life, as well as accounts of reunions between long lost parties, such as the woman in Somerset and her brother.

The column would be interactive with its readers, a component of the paper designed to provide a valuable service to them, but also with the potential to pull in colourful human-interest vignettes which could entertain. And it would all kick off with a full-page feature on Gill Whitley and her husband John.

As a then member of the *Daily Mail*'s features department, the assignment to write the feature was given to me, and in early 1999 I travelled up from London to the chilly and windswept island of Anglesey to interview the Whitleys. Friendly and helpful, they were down-to-earth people who lived in a cluttered home in Holyhead, surrounded by their children and their pets. Yet theirs was a tale brimming with human drama and surmounted adversity.

I came back and wrote the story. But, frustratingly for me, it sat around for another few months awaiting final arrangements for the proposed weekly column, which I was now told would also fall within my domain.

To be frank, I was not very pleased about this. I was already writing the *Mail*'s '20 Years Ago ... ' column, which ran five days a week. I had been producing it for more than two years, and while it was an enjoyable (not to mention educational) endeavour, it required extensive research and was therefore time-consuming. It left considerably less time for my main interest of feature-writing, which – need I add? – involved more glamour, more razzmatazz and bigger by-lines. If I were to take on another column (albeit a weekly, not a daily one), I'd be squeezed even more. I agonised over this.

But the reality is that if you work for a major national newspaper, you are ill-advised to say no to the Editor. And that applies doubly to the *Daily Mail* and milord Dacre. So I graciously accepted the commission of this innovative new slot in the paper. And innovative it certainly was. There had always been 'missing persons' adverts, as well as 'where are they now?' features pondering the fate of those who had once been in the public eye and now languished in obscurity. But to my knowledge there had never before been a wide-ranging undertaking such as this in any newspaper or magazine.

(I have since learnt of two people-tracing newspaper columns which pre-dated the *Mail*'s, by a long way. In 1886 *Lloyds Weekly*, in London, launched the Long-Lost Relatives column which published details of Brits who had emigrated to Australia, New Zealand, America and elsewhere and were being sought by their families back home. As the paper put it, the column expressed 'the earnest desire of many parents to hear from sons and daughters scattered abroad'. It added that they would not, however, deal with cases of 'runaway husbands'. And from 1831 to 1921 the *Boston Pilot* published Missing Friends, a column which published adverts from people looking for friends and relatives who had emigrated from Ireland to America – most of them itinerant navvies following construction jobs as they came up on the railroads and canals.)

By the early summer of 1999 the *Daily Mail* was finally ready for blast-off with the Missing and Found column, and the first one appeared on Saturday 26th June, followed a few days later by my article introducing the Whitleys to our readers. As the *Mail* explained, the paper would be working in association with the Anglesey couple to try to locate readers' missing friends and estranged loved ones. (As it turned out, the long-running '20 Years Ago . . . ' column came to its natural end – okay, it was killed off – earlier the same month. I suddenly had more time on my hands and stopped agonising about taking on the new column.)

The intention was to publish 'missing' stories in the hope that the *Mail*'s mass-circulation publicity would lead to the where-abouts of the individuals being sought, while Gill worked actively to trace people behind the scenes. We reckoned that at first we would need to rely quite heavily on Gill's diligent backroom endeavours, aided, of course, by her husband John. But we sincerely expected that, as the column gradually gained greater visibility in the paper and a wider audience through word-of-mouth, most of 'the lost' would be found through the particularly long reach of the *Daily Mail* itself. And that is precisely what happened. It is satisfying to know that, in many cases, Missing and Found has located the missing when even the mighty Friends Reunited and the venerable Salvation Army have come up empty-handed. That's the power of the press, God bless it.

*   *   *

Daily Mail, Thursday, 1 July 1999

THE FINDERS

On Saturday, the *Mail* launched a 'Missing' and 'Found!' column, to highlight people searching for lost relatives or friends. We enlisted the help of husband and wife team Gill and John Whitley, who have become expert at reuniting estranged relatives ever since they tracked down John's long-lost mother Doreen. Here, they tell MONICA PORTER about their own emotional search.

One day four years ago, John Whitley was at home watching television when the telephone rang. At the other end of the line was a woman with an unfamiliar voice. 'I'm your mother,' she said bluntly.

First shocked, then sceptical, John replied: 'No you're not.' But the woman went on to give John such details about his childhood that he was finally convinced he really had found his long-lost mother.

That extraordinary moment was the culmination of a long and often frustrating search by John and his wife Gill for the mother he had not seen in thirty-four years.

But while it was the end of his search, it sparked the beginning of a remarkable crusade. From their terrace house in Holyhead on the Isle of Anglesey, John and Gill have since brought happiness to seventy divided families, often simply by writing letters and making phone calls.

It is all part of the service they decided to set up, Searching For A Memory, which is funded by private donations. The Whitleys are now working on another forty or so cases.

It can take them months to find someone, or only two hours.

Daily Mail, Thursday, July 1, 1999

FEMAIL SPECIAL REPORT

THE FINDERS

The couple behind our Missing and Found column on their own search for a long-lost relative

ON SATURDAY, the Mail launched a 'Missing' and 'Found!' column, to highlight people searching for lost relatives or friends. We enlisted the help of husband and wife team Gill and John Whitley, who have become expert at reuniting estranged relatives ever since they tracked down John's long-lost mother Doreen. Here, they tell MONICA PORTER about their own emotional search.

O NE day four years ago, John Whitley was at home watching television when the telephone rang. At the other end of the line was a woman with an unfamiliar voice. 'I'm your mother,' she said bluntly.

First shocked, then sceptical, John replied: 'No you're not.' But the woman went on to give John such details about his childhood that he was finally convinced he really had found his long-lost mother.

That extraordinary moment was the culmination of a long and often frustrating search by John and his wife Gill for the mother he had not seen in 34 years.

But while it was the end of his search, it sparked the beginning of a remarkable crusade. From their terrace house in Holyhead on the Isle of Anglesey, John and Gill have since brought happiness to 70 divided families, often simply by writing letters and making phone calls.

It is all part of the service they decided to set up, Searching For A Memory, which is funded by private donations. The Whitleys are now working on another 40 or so cases.

It can take them months to find someone, or only two hours. 'Sometimes a single phone call will do it,' says Gill. 'Other times we have to try everything — tax offices, electoral rolls, the Office of National Statistics.

'We've done stake-outs, waiting for people to turn up, and once in a while the police give us an unofficial nudge in the right direction. We've even done broadcasts on pirate radio stations.'

Most helpful of all, according to John, are the general public. 'People are naturally curious and like to help whenever they can. They're happy to give you bits of information about somebody they know.'

The Whitleys have been married for 22 years and have eight children between them — four their first marriages and four together. They can't afford many luxuries but they provide their big brood with something

John himself saw little of as a child — parental devotion. His parents were alcoholics, his explains, and his father had a reputation for violence.

Taken into care at the age of 12, John grew to resent the mother who never came to visit him. He saw her only once, briefly, before he left the children's home at 15.

'My father told me she'd run off with another man,' he says. 'I had worshipped her as a small child and I felt she'd betrayed me.'

John drifted from job to job, developed a drink problem of his own and got into frequent fights. His life seemed aimless until, at 27, he met Gill, a 29-year-old divorcee.

'John had a reputation for being wild,' she recalls, 'but I believe in making up my own mind about people and I could see the real person beneath the bravado. I knew that with patience, understanding and perseverance I could draw him out.'

The meeting was to change John's life. 'Gill gave me what I had always wanted — stability, real love and caring. Gill was the first to treat me like a human being, and she put me on the straight and narrow.'

It was Gill who, five years ago, encouraged him to find his mother, Doreen. 'I knew he would never be at peace with himself until he had laid the ghosts of the past.'

At first they had no idea how to set about the quest, and simply felt their way along. Records from John's old children's home

provided them with the name she had assumed on 'abandoning' her family decades before. And John remembered the city of Bradford came into her life. It was a starting point.

Before long they had tracked down an uncle who was living in Chester, but he knew nothing of his sister's whereabouts.

T HEY decided to place a letter in a Bradford newspaper — and just two hours later John received that fateful phone call from his mother. It turned out that she had been reading the paper every day for years, hoping that one of her children would be looking for her.

John and Gill travelled to Bradford for an initial encounter with Doreen in a working men's club. 'I was petrified,' admits John. 'I expected to find an attractive young woman with long, black hair — that's how I remembered her. Instead there was an old woman, white-haired and stooped.

'But even so, I recognised my mother right away. I looked at her and said, a bit nervously: "Hello, darling."'

Doreen cried out, 'It's our John!' and tears flowed down

her cheeks. John tried to keep his emotions under control, but they soon got the better of him and he, too, began to weep. For a few emotional moments they could barely speak. Then they started talking — 'and there was no stopping them', says Gill.

John says: 'All the hatred and resentment I'd felt for so long just melted away. I realised that, underneath it all, I had always loved her. It was almost as if I was that 12-year-old boy again.'

And at last he learned the truth: his mother had not 'run off' with a lover but had disappeared because she was frightened of her violent husband. She had tried to hold on to her children but the authorities had insisted they be taken into care.

Sadly, Doreen had terminal cancer, but for the last two months of her life she moved in with the Whitleys and was surrounded by a loving family.

For John, it was as if the one vital piece of his life which had always been missing was finally put into place. 'You can't put a price on that,' he says. 'It's better than winning the Lottery.'

■ IF THERE is someone you would like to trace, write to Gill Whitley, 58 Tan-yr-efail, Holyhead, Anglesey, LL65 2SD. Or send an e-mail to monica.porter@dailymail.co.uk

John and Gill Whitley, and his mother Doreen, right, with great granddaughter Charlotte

The couple behind our 'Missing and Found' column on their own search for a long-lost relative:

13

'Sometimes a single phone call will do it,' says Gill. 'Other times we have to try everything – tax offices, electoral rolls, the Office for National Statistics.

'We've done stake-outs, waiting for people to turn up, and once in a while the police give us an unofficial nudge in the right direction. We've even done broadcasts on pirate radio stations.'

Most helpful of all, according to John, are the general public: 'People are naturally curious and like to help whenever they can. They're happy to give you bits of information about somebody they know.'

The Whitleys have been married for twenty-two years and have eight children between them – four from their first marriages and four together. They can't afford many luxuries but they provide their big brood with something John himself saw little of as a child – parental devotion. His parents were alcoholics, he explains, and his father had a reputation for violence.

Taken into care at the age of twelve, John grew to resent the mother who never came to visit him. He saw her only once, briefly, before he left the children's home at fifteen.

'My father told me she'd run off with another man,' he says. 'I had worshipped her as a small child and I felt she'd betrayed me.'

John drifted from job to job, developed a drink problem of his own and got into frequent fights. His life seemed aimless until, at twenty-seven, he met Gill, a twenty-nine-year-old divorcee.

'John had a reputation for being wild,' she recalls, 'but I believe in making up my own mind about people and I could see the real person beneath the bravado. I knew that with patience, under-standing and perseverance I could draw him out.'

Their meeting was to change John's life: 'Gill gave me what I had always wanted – stability, real love and caring. Gill was the first to treat me like a human being, and she put me on the straight and narrow.'

It was Gill who, five years ago, encouraged him to find his mother, Doreen. 'I knew he would never be at peace with himself until he had laid the ghosts of the past.'

At first they had no idea how to set about the quest, and simply felt their way along. Records from John's old children's home provided them with the name she had assumed on 'abandoning' her family decades before. And John remembered the city of Bradford came into her life somehow. It was a starting point.

Before long they had tracked down an uncle who was living in Chester, but he knew nothing of his sister's whereabouts.

They decided to place a letter in a Bradford newspaper – and just two hours later John received that fateful phone call from his mother. It turned out that she had been reading the paper every day for years, hoping that one of her children would be looking for her.

John and Gill travelled to Bradford for an initial encounter with Doreen in a working men's club. 'I was petrified,' admits John. 'I expected to find an attractive young woman with long, black hair – that's how I remembered her. Instead there was an old woman, white-haired and stooped.

'But even so, I recognised my mother right away. I looked at her and said, a bit nervously: "Hello, darling".'

Doreen cried out, 'It's our John!' and tears flowed down her cheeks. John tried to keep his emotions under control, but they soon got the better of him and he, too, began to weep. For a few emotional moments they could barely speak. Then they started talking – 'and there was no stopping them,' says Gill.

John says: 'All the hatred and resentment I'd felt for so long just melted away. I realised that, underneath it all, I had always loved her. It was almost as if I was that twelve-year-old boy again.'

And at last he learned the truth: his mother had not 'run off' with a lover but had disappeared because she was frightened of her violent husband. She had tried to hold on to her children but the authorities had insisted they be taken into care.

The first column, 26 June 1999

MISSING

THIS WEEK, in our new-look Coffee Break, the Daily Mail is offering readers a unique service to help people re-establish contact with old friends or relatives. Aiding us in this new weekly column will be Gill and John Whitley who, following their own search for John's long-lost mother, have become experts at reuniting estranged friends and family. Every week MONICA PORTER will feature the story of someone who is trying to find a loved one, and a tale of people reunited. To start looking for someone, or help find a missing loved one, see the foot of the page.

CLAIRE SIMPSON, 32, grew up in Batley, West Yorkshire, one of seven children whose father was a building foreman for the local council.

At the age of ten she befriended Anthony Todd, also ten, in her class at school. He lived in a children's home close to Claire's family home.

'He was a nice, lively child who was always joking,' Claire reminisces.

'We had a lot of laughs. His parents had separated, but he didn't seem affected by his unhappy family background.

'We became best friends and spent all our weekends together, playing the usual children's games — hide 'n' seek, the swings, running around in the fields.

'We were so close. I visited him a lot at the Cottage Homes, where he lived. It was a massive home, with loads of children, but the people who ran it were friendly and always made me welcome.

'It was a really happy time for both of us. But it only lasted about a year.'

One day Anthony didn't appear at school, so that afternoon Claire went to the home to find him. But he was gone. She was told that his father had come up from London and taken him away. That was at the end of the Seventies, and she never saw him again. Claire finished her school days with-

A childhood picture of Claire

out her best friend. At 23, she married a local man, a printer who worked in a family business, but they divorced two years ago. She has two sons at primary school — John, seven, and Josh, six — and spends most of her time caring for them.

But she has continued to think back fondly of the young boy with whom she had shared a special bond.

'I can still picture us together so clearly. I'd love to meet him again. I just want to know what happened to him after his father took him away so suddenly. Is he married? Does he have children?

'I want to know where he is and what his life is like, and if he's happy. I'd just like to know that he is safe and to tell him that I haven't forgotten him.'

Sadly, Doreen had terminal cancer, but for the last two months of her life she moved in with the Whitleys and was surrounded by a loving family.

For John, it was as if the one vital piece of his life which had always been missing was finally put into place. 'You can't put a price on that,' he says. 'It's better than winning the Lottery.'

FOUND!

Together at last: Glenys, left, with half-sister Shirley

GLENYS JEFFS is a 55-year-old Shropshire housewife. She was born on the Isle of Wight to a woman having an affair while her husband was abroad fighting in the war, and was given up for adoption to avoid scandal.

Brought to the mainland, Glenys was brought up in the Midlands, at the heart of a loving adoptive family.

In recent years she has longed to contact her natural mother. All she had to go on were her adoption papers, naming her mother as Violet Constable.

Her inquiries led nowhere, so she contacted our 'missing person' researchers, Gill and John Whitley. An appeal on an Isle of Wight radio station brought a response from a family friend of the Constables.

Gill learned that, although her natural mother Violet had died in 1992, Glenys had two older half-sisters living on the island. Gill phoned them both.

They were shocked to discover the existence of their unknown relative.

They had heard vague rumours about their mother's wartime 'love child', but had not really believed them.

One of the sisters, Shirley, was delighted to learn of her unknown sister. Right away she rang Glenys — who was equally thrilled — and the two had a long talk.

By coincidence, both had four children. But Shirley was divorced and had had a more troubled life than her illegitimate half-sister — their mother's 'dark secret'. Shirley helped put together the jigsaw of Glenys's earliest days.

Shirley and Glenys have become great friends. They have met several times. Shirley remarried recently, and Glenys was a witness at the wedding. They plan to see in the millennium together with a big, extended family party.

■ *IF THERE is someone you would like to trace, write to Monica Porter, c/o Missing/Found! The Daily Mail, Northcliffe House, 2 Derry Street, London W8 5TT. Fax No 0171-937 2471. Or send an e-mail to monica.porter@dailymail.co.uk This column is researched with the aid of the Info-Disk database of UK residents. 0800 980 7100.*

CHAPTER TWO

A Twenty-first Century Industry

Reunions between long-separated friends, schoolmates, university chums, army buddies, work colleagues, family members and so on, constitute a veritable industry in the twenty-first century. It has been powered chiefly by the internet and its burgeoning network of websites designed for the purpose.

This book's sub-title might seem a tad boastful – for which, please excuse me – but when the Missing and Found column was launched in the summer of 1999, it was undeniably in the vanguard of this movement. The hugely successful Friends Reunited website, the first and foremost of the genre to appear online in the UK, arrived a year later in 2000. It was followed soon after by the rest of the herd: Classmates Reunited, Forces Reunited, Genes Reunited, Tracesmart, UK People Finder, Find My Past and countless others, some for general consumption, some specialising in certain sectors, some allowing free searches of records and archives, while others charge a fee to access a database and online community.

How much influence did the *Daily Mail*'s column have on the propagation of all this reunion activity? It would be difficult to say, as this sort of popular movement develops organically, rather than in a linear fashion. No doubt it did play a part. In any case, one thing is for sure: the influence wasn't the other way around!

While it's true that the US-based website Classmates.com was launched as early as 1995, few people in Britain had heard of it back in the late Nineties, when only a small proportion of the population used the internet. (Although the site became known to the computer programmers who devised Friends Reunited, which is loosely modelled on it.)

Perhaps it was purely fortuitous that our column kicked off just as Britain was ready to launch into this new social phenomenon. But I don't believe so. I think its timing was prescient. Our editors picked up on a certain mood of the era, created by a combination of two important factors. Firstly, the emergence of the World Wide Web and the e-mail revolution had begun to make the world smaller, to bring people together and give even private individuals more public visibility. And secondly, in 1999, being on the brink of a new millennium was creating not only excited conjecture about what the future would bring, but thoughtful reflection on the past. It was a turning point – both in the history of our civilisation, and as many people perceived it, in their personal lives. Reconnecting with one's own past somehow fell naturally into the pervading spirit of that time. Thus the reunion industry was born.

Before long the column became a well-read spot in the paper. I certainly can't recall any period when there was a shortage of readers asking me to run their stories about the long lost people they hoped to find. Fairly early on the number of e-mails and letters I received reached 25 to 30 per week, and it has remained at that level ever since.

Of course, there had to be 'Found' in the column each week, as well as a 'Missing'. And for the first year or so my Founds were produced mainly by the good offices of Gill Whitley. Every month she would send me a list of her latest reunion successes and I would choose from among them. The idea was to have a good 'mix' of stories – rather as the paper itself likes to mix 'n' match articles in each issue so as to balance the subject matter and create a counterpoint between the serious and the light-hearted.

But with time, more and more of the 'missing' were found by virtue of their appearance in the column. Not everyone reads the *Daily Mail*, of course (although a great many do), but everyone knows someone who *does* read it. Even those who are most sniffy about the paper, e.g. subscribers to the *Guardian* and members of the Arthur Scargill appreciation society, will have a neighbour or a cousin or a sister-in-law who takes the *Mail*. So if your name and photo appear in it – even in a small column towards the back – someone who knows you is likely to see it and bring it to your attention.

One development in the life of the column which I did not predict has been the number of websites referring to it, citing its success rate and advising members to make use of it. The Veterans UK site, for example, has put quite a few former servicemen my way. It has also cropped up in the blogosphere, in forum chats about missing-friend searches. All this has meant that a sizeable proportion of the people who now ask me to feature their stories aren't even *Daily Mail* readers . . . not to start with, anyway.

It has always been a source of real regret to me that, inevitably, I have to turn so many people down. Here are the maths: I have space to use one 'Missing' story a week, yet each week, as I mentioned, I receive approximately 25–30 potential stories. So I need to be highly selective. I aim to feature an interesting variety of story types and themes, pegged to a variety of periods (although the majority relate to the 1950s, '60s or '70s), and generally choose the ones with a good chance of a successful outcome – as well as a nice picture to go with it. Sometimes – call me an old softie – I'm so moved by a particularly plaintive appeal that I feel compelled to say yes. And I should add that I'm rather more receptive to well-composed and heartfelt missives than to slapdash or curt ones. But other than that, quite honestly, it is a bit luck-of-the-draw.

The vast majority of people understand this and graciously accept that I'm unable to take on every request – and I always offer a long list of alternative people-finding avenues for them to explore. But on a few rare occasions I have received an irate rejoinder berating me for turning the correspondent down while the footnote at the end of the column each Saturday invites readers to send in their requests. I can sympathise with their annoyance. My only answer is that Missing and Found should be regarded as an exercise akin to the 'Letters to the Editor' page in any newspaper. There, too, readers are routinely invited to send in their letters. But only a small fraction of them ever appear in print.

Missing and Found, it seems, is a victim of its own success!

Many *Mail* readers tell me that they turn to the column every week out of curiosity to see if anybody they know is featured in it. If suddenly a name or face they recognise leaps out at them from the page, they are suitably delighted. And you can imagine how much greater the surprise if the face peering out at them is their own. It has happened often enough.

But in my view there is another aspect to the column which is equally appealing to readers and an important reason for its enduring popularity. While many of the stories it contains revolve around moving personal relationships – for instance a father's search for his estranged daughter – to which we can relate on a purely human, emotional level, many others are concerned with more than just the individuals named in them. They tap into our collective social and cultural memory. Whether it's a Second World War story or a tale pegged to the spirit and music of the Swinging Sixties, an account involving some well-remembered old name from the world of sport or showbiz or commerce, or a story linked to a major news event or episode from history, these are evocative narratives which resonate with the national psyche. In a way, they are really about us all.

CHAPTER THREE

In the Back Room

Q and A session with Gill Whitley

MP: How many successful reunions have you been able to bring about since you began your people-finding mission fourteen years ago?

GW: It's now more than 6,000, but I haven't got an exact figure. I'm afraid I had to dispose of a great many of the older files, because I ran out space for them.

MP: Is there any one category of search which dominates?

GW: The largest group is people looking for their friends, followed by people looking for relatives of one kind or another. Only a small percentage are adoption stories in which someone wants to find a birth parent, but these are my favourites because I was adopted myself and spent years trying to find the father I never knew. I drew a complete blank and it's too late now, because there's no one left alive who can tell me about him. I feel that reuniting other adoptees with their parents makes up for my own disappointment.

MP: How have your methods for finding people evolved over the years, with the advent of electronic databases and new resources available via the internet?

GW: At the onset John and I often resorted to stake-outs, which could get a little tricky. For example, once when finding a woman who had given up her baby boy for adoption some twenty-two years previously, we had to wait outside her house for hours to make sure we had the right person. While we waited one of the residents of the street got suspicious and called the police. When they arrived we explained what we were doing and fortunately they let us carry on. The end result of that search was that mother and son were happily reunited.

The names on the electoral roll databases available on CD Rom at that time were limited to the surnames and first initials of individuals. This meant that I often had to send out hundreds of letters to find the person I was seeking and it was very much hit-or-miss. The difference now is that the databases are more comprehensive and contain full names and in some cases even the date of birth and telephone numbers.

In the old days if I was searching for a woman and knew only her maiden name and her age, I would have to drive for forty minutes to the nearest big public library which had the birth, death and marriage records for England and Wales from 1837 to the present day. This was in order to discover her married name and the name of her husband. Searching through the microfiche records was very time-consuming, especially as they were often difficult to decipher. Sometimes it was necessary to go back a hundred years and many generations.

Now, with all the people-tracing websites available, it is much quicker and easier. Find my Past, which is the website I use most often, holds the same records for births, deaths and marriages as used to be held in Somerset House and the old Family Records Centre in London. I also use Facebook and Friends Reunited sometimes, as well as the

Tracesmart and 192 sites, which are based on the electoral roll, and other online records and directories.

MP: What developments do you predict with regard to people-tracing methodology?

GW: There's been worrying talk recently about the government possibly abolishing the edited register of the electoral roll. This is an invaluable resource for me, without which I couldn't do my work. It's the single most important database. I hope the government decides to keep it and allow public access to it, otherwise my job will get very difficult.

MP: As your work routine is now more desk-bound, do you find it less interesting and fulfilling?

GW: Not at all. Methods may have changed over the years, but the satisfaction I get from bringing about happy reunions remains the same as ever. If I were a lot younger I might miss the drama of the early days of Searching For A Memory, but now, at sixty-two, I don't mind it being a bit more sedentary.

MP: How much of your time do you spend on your searches?

GW: Normally about five or six hours a day. It depends on how much else is going on in my life. John and I have thirty grandchildren between us, at the last count, so things can get pretty hectic.

MP: How many searches do you have on the go at any one time?

GW: On average, about forty.

MP: What expenses are incurred in a search?

GW: Using Find my Past and other websites can prove costly if I need to order a number of certificates for births, deaths or marriages in order to move a search forward. Certificates cost about £14 each (about half that if you order them directly from the local register office where the records are kept). But first they charge for searching the records, which costs about £7 for ten searches, with each search looking through ten pages. Or you can take out an annual subscription which gives you unlimited access to the basic records for approximately £100. Costs can really add up for people-tracing novices who are unsure where to find information and might end up going all around the houses before they find what they are looking for. Then it could cost hundreds of pounds.

And of course I still have postage, stationery and telephone expenses.

MP: How involved these days is John in your search activities, and do you have others assisting you?

GW: John's not in good health now, so he doesn't get involved. But I have three ladies who assist me, working from their own homes: Carole in Bradford, Christine in East Sussex and Carolyn in Gwent, South Wales.

MP: What type of search is the most difficult to carry out?

GW: There is no one type which is most difficult. Whatever the nature of the search, it's impossible to predict how it will pan out. Sometimes it can look really easy but turn out to be hellish, at other times a search I expect to be a long, hard slog will fall into place very quickly, as if it was meant to be. The most difficult ones have taken me 18 months.

MP: How often do you abandon a search because you decide it is impossible to find the person being sought?

GW: Not very often, but there are some that prove fruitless and I have to give up, usually when the people being sought have gone abroad to live and there are no more family members left in the UK.

MP: Are there certain types of searches which you refuse to take on?

GW: Yes. I won't have anything to do with debt. If someone is looking for a person who owes them money, I'll refuse to help. Likewise if I get a sense that there is some aggression involved and the person being sought is in danger of getting hurt. The people I help have to be up-front with me and not be hiding anything.

I wouldn't search for anyone under eighteen, neither would I help an adopted child who is under 18 track down a birth parent because they're not legally entitled to do it before that age. I've had eleven and twelve-year-olds writing to me, asking me to find their birth mums. I feel sad for them, but I turn them away and tell them to come back when they're eighteen.

MP: Have you got an all-time favourite reunion story?

GW: If I have to choose one, it's probably the story of Vanessa Parkinson, from about 10 years ago. She'd been adopted as a baby and wanted to find her real mother. I managed to trace her mum, a lovely lady called Peggy, who was thrilled to have been found. She explained that she'd been an unmarried young girl when she fell pregnant with Vanessa and had no choice but to give her up at birth – that's the way things usually worked back in the fifties. But she told me that every day since then she'd wondered what had become of her daughter.

Vanessa lived in Lancashire and Peggy was in the south of England. They met up, and until Peggy's death earlier this year were in constant contact and as close as any mother and child could ever be. It was the closeness between them – as if they'd never been apart – that I found so moving.

MP: Do you often get emotionally drawn into the stories of the people you are helping?

GW: Inevitably I do get involved because I act as a kind of mediator between the two parties. There have been times when I've cried with people on the phone. It can be emotionally draining, but it's worth it.

MP: Do you remain in touch with many of the people you help to reunite? And if so, in your experience do the reunited stay in touch with each other, or do they lose contact again? What can go wrong?

GW: A number of them do stay in touch with me. I still get Christmas cards every year from some. But usually after a search is over I just move on to the next one, and they also move on with their lives. I know from occasional feedback I've had, though, that sometimes things do go wrong between reunited people. After a while they can fall out with each other. People can change a lot over a long period, so that it seems they are 'not the same person' any more. That can be very disappointing to the friend or relative who tried so hard to find them. I always advise people to keep an open mind, not to have too fixed an idea of what the person from long ago should be like today.

In one of the worst cases, I reunited a woman with her mother, who then tried to get off with her son-in-law. As you can imagine it caused all sorts of problems in that family. The son-in-law rang up to tell me he wished I'd never bothered to find his wife's missing mother, and I think she broke off contact with them in the end. Just as well.

MP: In which circumstances would you advise someone not to look for the person they want to find, but to let them live on only in their memories?

GW: If there had been a great deal of hostility in the past between the individuals concerned, I'll often suggest that they let sleeping dogs lie. Very often old animosities don't peter out with the passing of time, they just get stirred up again and cause more problems.

I will also suggest they leave it if I think it will definitely cause extreme emotional hurt to someone if they carry on. For example in the case of a woman who wants to find the child she gave up for adoption in her youth, but who has not told either her husband or her other children about the existence of the adopted child. These women have a fear that they will lose the love of their family if that child's existence is revealed, and causing real hurt is a big risk. In a case such as that, I would suggest that the idea is shelved. It is hard on the person searching but it's something they have to come to terms with. Of course, there are no hard and fast rules. I have known one instance of this exact situation when a mother went ahead, found her long-missing, secret son and revealed everything to her family, who welcomed the son. But it doesn't always work out that way.

Also, I would sometimes advise a person not to search for a long lost love who is likely to be in a relationship that would suffer as a result . . . although I *have* located lost loves who turned out to be widowed or divorced, and the two people concerned got together again and ended up marrying. Life never turns out the way you think it will.

In other cases, if I've already found the person who was being sought and they insist that they don't want to have contact with whoever was looking for them, I have to respect this and let the searcher know – as well as the reasons for the rejection, if I've been informed of them. People have a right to keep their past in the past, if that is what they want.

CHAPTER FOUR

All of Life

If variety is the spice of life, Missing and Found is a spicy little number. In the early days my favourite items revolved around some tale of wartime derring-do. A Spitfire pilot hoping to trace his fellow crew members in order to relive their glory days in the Battle of Britain, or an old soldier looking for the buddy with whom he went through hell on the Normandy beaches. More surprisingly, one of my favourite stories reunited a one-time British soldier with the captured German he had guarded and befriended in a POW camp on Guernsey.

A decade on, those stories are thinner on the ground, of course, as that wartime generation slowly fades out. But luckily we've still got some rollicking accounts coming in from the National Service boys who saw action in the 1950s in Korea, Suez, Malaya, Cyprus and other hotspots of the period. In fact National Service was clearly the premier male-bonding experience for British men now in their seventies; it seems they all want to get back together with their erstwhile mates-in-uniform, and happily I've helped many do just that. But I receive such a heavy volume of NS-related requests that I must ration them quite strictly, so as to leave some space for others.

Another major category involves those who were children during the war and still have vivid recollections, either of being evacuated to strangers' homes in the countryside or of belonging to some close-knit gang of neighbourhood kids with whom they shared memorable escapades – exploring bomb sites, watching aerial dog-fights, surviving air raids. Today's youngsters, with their 'virtual adventures' in video games and the passive excitements offered by TV, are unlikely to remember their childhood activities with the same degree of clarity or share such deep-rooted bonds with their playfellows.

The organisers of school and college reunions are keen users of the column (especially, for some reason, groups of nurses who did their training together). Needless to say, the school reunion is a whole world unto itself and the column has done its bit to increase the numbers at such gatherings.

At times I quite fancy being a fly on the wall to see what goes on. I've never been to a school reunion of my own, but some time ago my partner Nick attended the thirty-year reunion of his classmates from one of those English public schools which used to make boys' lives miserable and leave them with lifelong hang-ups. He was none too keen to attend the black-tie reunion dinner at his unloved Alma Mater – after managing successfully to stay away from the place since he was eighteen – but he did go in the end, out of curiosity. During the meal Nick sat beside the former pupil who had mercilessly bullied him for years, now overweight, balding and stuck in a boring job. And afterwards, Nick told me, 'as we got plastered together over our brandies, we had a truly profound, revelatory conversation . . . I think. I've forgotten most of it. But it doesn't matter, because the main thing is I managed to lay that old ghost to rest for good.'

So, a most beneficial outcome, once he had recovered from alcohol poisoning.

Through the column I discovered that we are an amazingly musical nation. I've received an inordinate number of requests from people in search of their fellow former members of pop groups, rock bands, dance bands, military bands, orchestras, jazz combos, skiffle groups and choirs. Some were professional musicians, some semi-professional and the rest unassuming amateurs, but their music-making was clearly of great significance to them all, as were their fellow music-makers.

Who could have guessed that quite so many 1960s youths traipsed around the country with guitars and drum sets, doing gigs, aspiring to the big time? The groovy groups we've featured over the years include the Phantoms, the Sabres, the Metropolitans, the Duty Crew, the Delcardoes, the Sat-Lytz, the Sentano Sextet and the Bojaks Garage Band. Oh, that other group of the era, the Beatles, has cropped up in the column too.

And we are no less sporty. Footballers, cricketers, rugby players, cyclists and boxers, athletes, hikers and swimmers and oarsmen have all made appearances in search of their erstwhile sporting compadres. And of course the members of countless clubs and organisations have featured – from the vast, such as the Boy Scouts, to the tiny, such as the Lucky 13 Scooter Club of south-east London.

Another major category in the column is former work colleagues. These days it is the norm to change jobs frequently, to keep 'trading up'. Employees – whether they work for City banks, law firms, media organisations or any other type of business – are not actually expected to remain loyal and committed to their employer indefinitely. More than ever before, it is assumed that as soon as a slightly rosier opportunity crops up, an employee will be off like a shot with nary a backward glance.

But it wasn't always like that. It is clear from the annals of Missing and Found that in bygone times many people felt strongly attached to the company they worked for, retaining a lifelong affection for it and for their colleagues. And this wasn't because they had a cushy time, with lots of perks and bonuses. There was simply a sense that a job could, and perhaps should, be 'for life', and that one's co-workers were a kind of family. That is why so many Missing-and-Founders, now in their sixties and seventies, are looking for their past colleagues, often from companies which no longer exist and whose names conjure up a whiff of the past for us, too. Anyone recall the quaintly-named Hunting Clan Air Transport, or the later British United Airways, the ABC Cinema chain or the once-mighty Elder Dempster Shipping Line of Liverpool?

The column has also enjoyed a goodly sprinkling of stardust from the showbiz fraternity. Obviously I'm not referring to those celebs who are rarely out of the papers or off the telly (they are the ones we'd dearly *love* to be missing, sometimes). I mean the less celebrated but still evocative faces and names from yesteryear. The film starlet who appeared in a handful of British comedies in the 1950s, the actor with a small part in the 1960s TV series The Saint and the tenor with a solo singing role in the film Oh What a Lovely War. The kids from the popular 1930s radio show, the Ovaltineys, and the long-retired but still lively variety-show comic. All of them now living quiet, private lives somewhere and being reconnected with long-lost friends and relatives via Missing and Found.

Apart from these major categories covered in the column, I have a particular penchant for the quirky one-off, the sort of little yarn which shows the British in all their glorious eccentricity. Into this grouping falls the Ancient & Honourable Order of Tibetian (sic) Layabouts, a 'mutual admiration society and the world's most secret jazz club', founded a half-century ago. We garnered five of its missing original members from various corners of the world for a grand reunion dinner.

And then there was Julie Smith, looking for her erstwhile friends from Neurotics Anonymous, a group she belonged to in the 1970s, which met in a London pub to discuss their phobias, relationship problems and other angst-ridden issues, 'with frequent intervals for topping up our drinks'. We put Julie in touch with Jackie (now living in the US), who had also been connected to the group.

Another of our stories concerned the well-known Loch Ness monster-hunter Frank Searle, once accused of faking photos of Nessie frolicking in the water, who suddenly vanished from the public eye in 1983. He was being sought by an old friend. Fortunately we were able to update his friend – and our readers – on his fate.

Assisting those who are researching for books of historical interest has been a gratifying sideline of the column. We located one of the last London trolleybus drivers for the writer of a book on British trolleybuses, and several individuals associated with the 6th Royal Scots Fusiliers for an erudite history of the battalion once commanded by Winston Churchill. But our greatest coup in this department was to find more than sixty people with personal memories of the 1961 Stavanger air crash (in which thirty-four British schoolboys died), for the writer of a book on the tragic event which made international headlines nearly fifty years ago.

As you can see the column has been fairly all-encompassing, with people from all walks of life, and transcending the class boundaries. Well, almost. I admit that the nobility has been largely absent, except for a Nigerian princess and the grand-sounding Lord Farcombe of Farcombe Hall, who claimed to live 'a dissolute life of idleness and pleasure' at his West Country manor. It all sounded like something out of an Evelyn Waugh novel, but his lordship soon admitted that his title was purely honorary, passed on to him by a (very distant) cousin in Canada.

I always tread warily when sensitive relationship matters crop up. For example, someone who had been taken into care as a child hoping to trace his mother or father. As we know, often these parents don't want to be 'found'. On the other hand, I believe it's perfectly understandable to want to know your parents, or who they were, and probably enshrined in the EU as a human right (everything else seems to be). It works the other way around too, of course, with a parent desperately seeking a child lost to misfortune decades earlier. We have featured many stories involving family break-up and abandonment. Often they result in a positive outcome, with a tearful reunion and celebratory drinks all round – rather like John Whitley's story. But sometimes the 'found' are uninterested and refuse to have their present lives and relationships ruffled by a ghost from the past. So after fishing them out of obscurity, you must take them off the hook so they can quietly swim away again.

'Old flame' scenarios require equally delicate handling. They can work out to everyone's satisfaction, as two such stories in the next chapter illustrate. But to be honest, often I prefer to leave them alone. We've all heard those well-publicised cautionary tales of marriages wrecked when a pair of old flames reconnect via the internet.

Early on in the column – the first few months, I think – I ran a story regarding a man in his fifties who, as a young soldier, had a brief but passionate affair with a beautiful girl he had never forgotten. He had gone on to marry someone else, was now divorced, and yearned to find that girl again. Maybe she was single, too, he reckoned, and just *maybe* they could rekindle that old fire. We used a picture of him in his early twenties, looking dapper in army uniform.

He was ecstatic and couldn't thank me enough when I e-mailed to tell him that she had made contact. It was one of my first successes and I was pretty thrilled myself. I put them in touch with each other and they arranged to meet up for a drink. I imagined them falling into each other's arms after thirty years and walking hand-in-hand into the sunset.

But of course it didn't happen that way, because we don't live in a Meg Ryan movie. Sometime after the ex-soldier and his old flame had their get-together (at a hotel in the Midlands, as I seem to recall) I e-mailed him to ask how it went and get the low-down for my follow-up Found item. He sent a very doleful-sounding reply. She was still good-looking, he informed me, and by a miracle she, too, was recently divorced and so was 'available' again. But not, apparently, available to him. They had talked for a long time and consumed a lot of drinks, but at the end of it all she announced that while he was a lovely guy and she was really fond of him, she wanted only to be friends. The oldest of old chestnuts.

It always made me wonder, that sad little tale, whether the ex-soldier wouldn't have done better not to search for his lost damsel at all. If he had never looked for her and we had never found her, she would have remained forever a distant, warming memory from his youth, a bittersweet, better-to-have-loved-and-lost experience. As it was, he'll remember her as the middle-aged divorcee who rejected him in a Midlands hotel after he spent a fortune on booze.

*　　*　　*

The wonderful thing about Missing and Found is that it's a little law unto itself. It works, as they say, in mysterious ways. It can locate a sought-after old friend who vanished decades earlier, in a single morning. Or it can take a couple of years. Some of the Found items relate to Missing stories which had been lying so long in the 'cold case files' that I had forgotten all about them. Apparently some readers, if they know the person being sought in a particular story, will cut out the column and keep it until the opportunity arises to do something about it. And often the route from A to B – or in this case from M to F – is long-winded and circuitous, involving, as it were, several 'degrees of separation'.

Unsurprisingly, it happens often enough that a person being looked for after several decades as a 'missing' is no longer alive. The search is too late. It is sad and disappointing when this happens, perhaps at times bitterly so. But at least the searcher can draw a line under that particular relationship, that episode in their life. There is something to be said for closure.

In many cases the column operates on a tangent. Either instead of, or in addition to, the individual or people being sought, it will produce a wholly different batch. Old chums, neighbours, work-mates, cousins and all manner of folk suddenly appear like so many rabbits out of hats.

Another by-product of the column – and a particularly fortunate one for me as a journalist – is that every so often a story falls into my lap via a Missing request which I realise has the makings of a full-blown feature article.

One such story involved the hundredth anniversary last year of the birth of British aviation in 1909 on the Isle of Sheppey. I was asked to locate descendents of the 'fathers of aviation' who had been instrumental in that first flight, undertaken by the dashing young trailblazer J. T. C. Moore-Brabazon (later Lord Brabazon of Tara) in his bi-plane, the Bird of Passage. A grand celebration was planned to mark the event on the original site of the flight and it was hoped that these descendents could attend. Happily, the item in the column found some relatives of the Short brothers, who set up the world's first aircraft factory on Sheppey and built Brabazon's plane. And I was inspired to research in detail that fascinating episode of British history and write an 1800-word magazine piece on it . . . before having an enjoyable day out myself at the anniversary celebration.

An unusual and poignant human-interest story which landed on my desk courtesy of the column also found a more expansive home in the pages of a magazine. Christine Brody's parents became estranged even before she was born and she was prevented from having a relationship with her father by a bitter and vindictive mother.

She grew up being told that her father wanted nothing to do with her, whereas in fact he had not only written to her regularly but even paid for a private education for her, which she never received. Christine's mother had withheld both the letters and the money. She even wrote back to her father, pretending to be Christine and putting him off from ever seeing her. As a result her father vanished abroad and now, five decades later, she had no idea where he was or whether he was still alive. It was a painful irony to Christine that she had spent a lifetime fostering children from broken homes, helping many to reunite with their parents, yet had been denied the same sort of closure herself.

The publicity brought her search to an end and helped secure that much-needed closure. Christine learned when and where her father had died, and found previously unknown relatives from his side of the family who could tell her more. 'You gave me a past, a history, as well as a present family. You wrought a miracle,' Christine wrote in her last message to me.

When I hear people disparaging the Press – a common pastime these days, and often fully justified – I like to remember the little 'miracles' such as these which it can achieve. They may not count for much in the grand sweep of human history, but are of incalculable worth to individual human beings.

*   *   *

I admit I sometimes get the feeling we've all gone reunion mad in recent years. Old friends and acquaintances constantly seek each other out on Facebook and Friends Reunited and elsewhere in the cyber-sphere. They Google each other. I myself get bombarded with e-mails from the hard-sell Classmates.com urging me to reconnect (for a fee) with people I went to high school with in Hartsdale, New York, a million years ago and haven't heard a dickey-bird from since.

Why is the reunion so important to us? Obviously, it's at least partly to do with the desire to recapture lost youth and vanished, simpler times through the long-lost people who connect us to them . And perhaps also, in this era of uncertainty and change, it's about our (possibly subconscious) search for self-validation. No friend knows us as well as an old friend, or so we believe.

We also like to gauge how well we've done in life against the yardstick of other people's fortunes. Witness another reunion which my partner Nick attended a couple of years ago. A friend with whom he grew up in Berkshire organised a get-together for their old crowd – boys and girls who used to hang out as teenagers at the home of the local vicar's son. The vicar and his wife had been a good-hearted, hospitable couple who welcomed their son Jim's pals at any time, and always with generous quantities of food – the ideal of the warm family home. Jim's kind and caring parents didn't send *him* off to some Victorian-style boarding school to be bullied and made miserable and left with hang-ups which would dog him for years to come. Lucky Jim.

The reunion was held at a cosy country pub in Berkshire and the long-lost friends greeted each other with hugs and hoots. A once-wild mate who'd been expelled from school for blowing up the playing field with a pipe bomb was now working in the insurance business. A once-winsome girl famed for her great legs and mini-skirts was now a jowly grandmother with a dodgy hip. And a fellow who'd had a reputation for boorishness was still just as boorish.

And then there was Jim. Seeing his old friend again after a gap of nearly three decades, Nick asked for an update on his life. The vicar's son took a slug of his gin-and-tonic. Wearily, he gave his answer: 'Three wives, three divorces, three kids, no money.'

Speechless, Nick did the only sensible thing. He ordered more drinks.

*   *   *

In the selection of seventy-five found items which follow, dated and accompanied by their original photographs, you will notice that there are none from before 2002. The first three years of the column's existence are missing. I apologise for this. The reason is that my electronic archive doesn't stretch back to the earliest years. Those stories survive only in the cuttings and in most cases it would now be very difficult, if not impossible, to retrieve the photos needed to illustrate them. But anyway, I reckon that seventy-five is plenty to be getting on with..

CHAPTER FIVE

Found!

1

12 December, 2009

Ronnie (far left) and Cyril (second from left)
in Hackney Boys' Club in the forties

Last month eighty-two-year-old Ronnie Frankel, who still runs a badminton school in Cockfosters, Hertfordshire, was looking for fellow members of a wartime boys' club – the Hackney Boys' Club in Martello Street in East London. He wrote: 'The club helped me greatly in my desire to be a PE instructor. I passed all the tests and worked in evening institutes for the London County Council until I was called up.

'Most of my pals from the club became Bevan Boys and went down the mines for their wartime service, but I decided to join the RAF. As I was already trained for it, I became a physical training instructor and stayed on longer than the original two years, eventually being promoted to sergeant.' He added that if there were more boys' clubs around today, 'the country would benefit enormously'. Well, you won't get an argument out of me.

Amongst the old pals Ronnie hoped to find was Cyril Goldberg, who was quick to respond with a cyber-missive: 'I am Cyril Goldberg, now known as Cyril Gee, and I'd like to make contact with Ronnie and any of the other lads. I have very happy memories of the Hackney Boys' Club.' And he goes on to tell us: 'I left school at fourteen to work at a music publishers in London, and at eighty-one I'm still in the music business. In 1958 I became MD of Mills Music, which later merged with another publisher to form Belwin-Mills Music, and I was MD for the new company. We were involved in all aspects of music, and at one time employed a young lad called Reg Dwight, now better known as Elton John . . . '

2

25 July 2009

In May Angela Lane, a teacher at the Percy Shurmer Primary School in Balsall Heath, Birmingham, sent in an unusual request. 'Our school is named after the much-loved MP for Sparkbrook in Birmingham, who did much to improve the lives of ordinary people in the area and died in 1959. He forced landlords to build proper sheds for dustbins, campaigned to have gas lights

*Percy Shurmer leading a sing-song
for the Sparrows in the fifties*

put in every yard and replaced the old block leaded ranges with
gas stoves.

'He also gave parties for poor children at Birmingham Town
Hall. These children were nicknamed the "Sparrows". At these
parties Percy Shurmer would lead the children in a jolly sing-
song. His fundraising also supported the St Martin's and
Deritend Girls' percussion band, the Shipwrecked Mariners'
Royal Benevolent Society and the elderly at Yardley Green
Sanatorium. I'm looking for any of his erstwhile Sparrows and
anyone else who knew him or benefited from his great work, so
they can attend the unveiling in June of a blue plaque in his
honour at the school which bears his name.'

Compared to most of today's MPs, Mr Shurmer was a veritable
saint. So we're happy that our item got a good result. Angela
reports: 'Your article was brilliant. Eleven people, including
several of the Sparrows, got in touch and of these four attended
last month's unveiling. Many thanks for that.'

3

28 November 2009

Peter Gold at eighteen

A month ago businessman Stewart Shaw was searching for an important friend from the sixties, Peter Gold. At that time Stewart was 'a depressed adolescent with an abusive father', living in North London and going to Woodberry Downs Comprehensive School. He was shy, lonely and unhappy. 'Then one day along came a bright boy my own age who was outgoing, friendly, and didn't give a fig for authority. His name was Peter Gold and he befriended me. Suddenly my life changed from a grey, sad existence to one that sparkled with adventure and happiness. I never looked back.'

Soon after leaving school, however, life pulled them apart and they lost touch. Stewart was keen to make contact again so he could thank Peter for what he did for him decades ago. Within a few days Peter got in touch, having been alerted to our column by a friend, and we reconnected the two men. Stewart updated us: 'Peter is retired, lives in East London and is busy in local politics. Still adventurous, he's off to India for three months in December, so we'll meet up when he's back. We're planning to go fishing together!

'I'd like to thank you and the *Daily Mail* for finding him. Just talking to him again, filling in those missing years and establishing that he is alive and well is a wonderful thing for me. Thanks also to my *Daily Mail*-reading friend June Young, who advised me to contact you in the first place.'

4

7 November 2009

There was an excellent response to Shane Litchfield's search last month for anyone who knew Leeds United footballer Grenville Hair, who died of a heart attack forty years ago, aged thirty-six. Shane is a good friend of Grenville's son Kenneth, who was only nine when his father passed away, but has always been very proud

Grenville Hair in his heyday

of him and keen to learn more about him. Now fifty, Ken lives in Repton, Derbyshire, where he sponsors local football and cricket. 'We've often discussed his dad,' wrote Shane, 'but the gaps in his knowledge are huge. Can you help?'

Bill Bell was the first of many to e-mail, from his present home in the US: 'Will you please give me the address of the young man looking for people who played with Grenville Hair, as I played with him at Leeds and would like to get in touch.' And this from Roy Wood: 'I was goalkeeper for Leeds from 1951 to 1960 and played in over 200 games with Grenville. He was a fine passer of the ball and was given the job of teaching me how to kick a dead ball from a goal kick.

'I remember once we were staying in a hotel in London the night before a match. One of the players rushed into reception, where the team's directors and manager were chatting, and shouted that Grenville had "a bird in his room". The manager angrily dashed up flights of stairs only to find a pigeon caught between the glass in the sash windows . . . '

And Geoff Illsley wrote to say: 'I was at school with Grenville in Newhall, South Derbyshire, and we delivered papers for the same newsagents in the High Street . . . '

Soon afterwards Ken Hair himself got in touch. 'I'd like to thank you personally for the opportunity to find out some unknown details about my late father. Initially I was shocked and annoyed that my friend Shane asked you to put in this article. I had no prior knowledge of it. But it resulted in all good news and a re-acquaintance with some long lost family friends – which placated my mother, who had also not been consulted before-hand. "If you need to know anything about your father, you ask me," was her response, days later. "What was the name of the lad who had a paper-round with Dad?" I asked. "I don't know,' she said. "Then you don't know everything about him, do you?" was my cheeky response.

'We have been overwhelmed by the stories from people who knew Gren. Although we lost him over forty years ago, he is still a local sporting hero. We've had contact from people who were involved with the same football clubs as my father, as well as from *Daily Mail* readers from Ireland, Madeira and Australia. Thanks again for allowing me to learn more about my father. We're very proud of him and of how his memory still contributes to our lives today.'

5

10 October 2009

A happy ending – at last – to a story we featured three years ago. Allan Bottomley told us then of his sad tale: 'While serving in the army in 1962, I met and married a girl called Joan from the WRAC. Soon afterwards I was posted to Germany and as we couldn't get married quarters there, she remained in England. The following year we had a daughter, Angela. Due to the distances involved, our marriage broke down and the parting was acrimonious. Joan

Allan as a young trooper in the 4th/7th Royal Dragoon Guards, 1963

simply disappeared with Angela. Then in the seventies Angela was adopted by Joan's new husband, with whom she moved to Canada. According to them, my daughter ceased to exist for me. But I never forgot or stopped caring about her.'

Now Allan has e-mailed with good news: 'As a result of your story a kind gentleman from Northern Ireland got in touch with advice on how to search for Angela. I did as much as I could before hitting a brick wall. But last March, the day before my sixty-fifth birthday, I received an e-mail from her. I nearly passed out when I read it. Apparently, at the age of sixteen she was told that the man she knew as her father had adopted her, but she was not told who her biological father was. Only last year, after her "dad's" death, was she finally told my name and the town I came from. She traced me through letters I'd written to the local paper.

'Angela lives 6000 miles away in the wilds of Canada. I have a grandson who has cerebral palsy but is a bright young lad all the same, and we are e-mailing daily and phoning every 10 days or so. As there is no NHS over there and my grandson is due for surgery and new callipers within the next couple of months, there is little spare cash for my daughter to get to England to see me. And as a disabled pensioner on the basics I can't afford to make the trip over there. However, I am deliriously happy that after forty-four years we have found each other. The rest is up to providence.'

6

3 October 2009

In August, Gerald 'Chalky' White of Lincoln was searching for fellow members of the voluntary Land Rescue Team attached to RAF Station Kai Tak in Hong Kong back in the early sixties. As he explained: 'We spent weekends visiting remote parts of the colony to locate water and helicopter landing sites, and to familiarise ourselves with the rocky terrain. We also gave up our spare time for training in map reading and abseiling.'

One of those being sought was Flight Lieutenant B. J. Lemon (known as Dink), who, whenever he was flying, would seek out the team's rescue lorry – which had a red cross painted on the roof – and buzz the vehicle in his jet-engined Venom aircraft, causing everyone to panic and duck. What jolly japes they had out East.

RAF rescue team, Hong Kong, 1960, with Dink leaning on walking stick, smoking a pipe

Chalky is pleased with the responses to his search. Ken Sims, another of the men he was looking for, said: 'I am very happy to renew acquaintance with my former Land Rescue Team mates, particularly Chalkie, who was my roommate.' And a helpful Brian Harding e-mailed: 'Until two years ago I worked for the Lord Roberts Workshops for Disabled Ex-service Personnel in Edinburgh. On the board of directors was ex-RAF Air Commodore Brian Lemon, about seventy years old, who flew Venom aircraft and had just the sort of daredevil personality to "buzz" his mates as described. He was intending to move to France from his home in Somerset. Brian is an absolutely cracking person and I'm sure would appreciate renewing old friendships.'

7

26 September 2009

Quentin Green, shortly before he died in the 1961 Stavanger air crash

Last month Rosalind Jones asked us to help locate relatives or friends of the thirty-four schoolboys and two teachers from Lanfranc School in Croydon who were killed in the Stavanger air crash of 1961. Three crew members from Eagle Airways also died when the plane crashed into the summit of a Norwegian mountain. As the first air crash involving so many children, it was a major news story. Rosalind's thirteen-year-old brother Quentin Green was one of those killed and she is writing a book about the tragedy to be published on its fiftieth anniversary in 2011. She wants to include as many personal memories as possible. Profits from the book will go to the Red Cross, in tribute to their work in retrieving the bodies from the mountain.

This item elicited a greater response than any other in the ten years of this column, and that's saying something. More than sixty people wrote in with their moving stories – relatives, friends, Lanfranc schoolmates and others with strong memories of the tragedy. One of them was Brian West: 'My cousin was one of the schoolboys who died and another relative was the plane's co-pilot that night, who had been on stand-by and took the place of the scheduled pilot who fell ill. His name was Murray Smalley, he had a young wife Nina and baby daughter . . . '

Ian Greest e-mailed: 'I was a Lanfranc boy at the time and got permission from my parents to go on that trip, but having reserved my place my father unfortunately lost his job and I had to stand down.' And we heard from Eddie Ottewell, who lost a lot of friends in the crash. His father was one of the local funeral directors who conducted the victims' mass funeral.' And that funeral was 'quite something to see', according to Glennis Cavanagh, a Lanfranc School pupil who knew three of the boys who died.'

Audrey Neale sent this message: 'My brother Charles Ella was at the school and scheduled to go on the trip to Norway. He was thirteen years old at the time. He ended up not going because he failed to save enough money in the period leading up to the trip. We were a large family (seven children) and my mother couldn't afford to pay. Many of those killed in the crash were classmates of my brother. He most likely knew Quentin Green and Dennis Field. When news of the accident first came through I remember how shocked we all were. My brother was very quiet, at his age he didn't really grasp the magnitude of the tragedy or his near-miss.'

Rosalind now has a wealth of new material for her book and we wish her the best of luck with it.

8

12 September 2009

Audrey and Ellen in Hyde Park in 1946

Last month Ellen Morgan, née Sharp, aged eighty-six, was looking for friends from the forties, with whom she worked at Chappell's Piano Company at 50 New Bond Street, in London's West End. Two colleagues she was particularly interested in were Audrey Baillie and Joyce Payne. 'We would often see celebrities at Chappell's, passing through the showroom on their way to the record and music department,' wrote Ellen. 'In later years Tom Jones and Engelbert Humper-dinck were often seen on the staircase, waiting for stardom.

'After the war I continued to work at Chappell's, but neither Joyce nor Audrey did. I lost touch with Joyce after she got married in 1944, and some time later Audrey moved abroad with her husband. She and I went to see the stage show of West Side Story together in 1958 and haven't had any contact since. It would be a dream come true if either she or Joyce were to get in touch. Chappell's was damaged by fire in 1963, but was repaired and I worked there until 1974. The company is now located in Ivor Novello's old house in Soho.'

Hooray, we've found both Joyce and Audrey. The three old friends are very happy to be back together again. And we've reconnected Ellen with eight other erstwhile colleagues, including Sue Phillips, who e-mailed: 'I worked for the director of the piano department at Chappell's and my great friend Christine worked as a cashier in the sheet music department. My boss Mr Hicks sported a wonderful Jimmy Edwards moustache. We worked in a little partitioned office off the great hall, which was filled with grand pianos, and when Tommy the blind piano tuner had done his work, the hall would resound with wonderful music. Walking down Bond Street recently I was disappointed to find No. 50 a building site. It was interesting to learn through your column where the company had moved to.'

9

29 August 2009

Last month Colin Dale, from Conwy in Wales, was searching for old mates from his pirate radio days in the sixties. He was closely associated with Screaming Lord Sutch and the Savages, having grown up in north London with the wacky David Sutch and worked as a disc jockey on Radio Sutch, which broadcast in 1964 from the Thames Estuary near Whitstable.

Danny McCulloch was first to respond with this e-mail: 'I played bass with the original Savages for eighteen months before the band left Dave and went to Germany, splitting up after a few years. After many moons of working the circuit with John Lee Hooker, Muddy Waters, Jerry Lee Lewis and Otis Reading, I joined The Animals. I'm writing a book about my life in the

Radio Sutch is launched on the Thames, May 1964

business and Dave Sutch is included in it.' We also heard from Nick Simper, who also played bass guitar for the Savages.

Then Janice Brett informed us that Savages' drummer Jack Irving and guitarist Angie Antinori, 'still perform and can usually be found at the jam night held every Monday at the New Chandos Pub in Colindale, north London. So Colin Dale might like to make a trip to Colindale.' And this from Angela Walton: 'My brother Fred Cheeseman was Dave Sutch's first piano player and went on to have a great career as Freddy Fingers Lee – a stage name invented for him by Dave. I remember when the band would stay at my mam's house on the way to gigs in Scotland. He was a funny man, was Sutchy. Fred no longer plays piano, but has good stories about his music days and lives in County Durham.' Finally, lead guitarist Geoff Mew also made contact; nowadays he trains pilots in the Middle East. Rock on!

10

15 August 2009

A couple of months ago Hugh Taylor of Edgware, Middlesex, was in search of a former London Transport trolleybus driver from the sixties, Adrian O'Callaghan. He was one of the last three conductors to be trained to drive trolleybuses at London's trolleybus driving school, and Hugh hoped to trace him so that he could include him in a book he's compiling about the conversion of the trolleybus routes to motorbus operation. Hugh has had a lifelong passion for trolleybuses and this is his fourth book on the subject.

He explained: 'The Edgware trolleybus terminus was right outside my infants school. The trolleybuses fascinated me and when I was old enough to venture around London on my own I decided to involve my-self with them. So I went to the Isleworth depot in west London, where I got to know the drivers, conductors and maintenance staff, who took me under their wing.'

In the photo he sent us Adrian, aged twenty-five, is standing with his conductor in front of trolleybus number No. 1274. As it was considered 'the smartest vehicle at Isleworth

Trolleybus driver Adrian O'Callaghan in Hounslow, 1962

depot', it was chosen to be the last to enter the depot on 9 May, 1962 – the last night of trolleybus operation in London.

Enter Adrian, who contacted us via a letter from his friend, Ms Bernadette Cafferty of Hatfield, Hertfordshire. Adrian himself lives in Colindale, north London, a mere two miles from Hugh, who updated us: 'Adrian and I met up on 30 June. I showed him a number of photos of his colleagues and he could identify many of them. Amazingly, he remembered me as the trolleybus-mad teenager who had photographed the Isleworth trolleybus staff in 1962. Many thanks, for publishing my request. I will now be able to include some of his anecdotes in my forthcoming book.'

11

8 August 2009

Michael Poole as Royal Marine during the Falklands War, 1982

Now for something different, my friends. Do you recall the story of Andrea Marono, from Argentina, who hoped to be reunited with Michael Poole, a Royal Marine seaman she met in Buenos Aires in February 1982, shortly before the outbreak of the Falklands War? Of course you do. Nicknamed Spike, Michael served on the HMS *Endurance* at Mar del Plata, near Buenos Aires. He and Andrea met at a bar and for a few weeks they had a lovely time together.

'I was very young,' Andrea reminisced, 'only sixteen, and he was twenty-six. He came home to have dinner with my parents, we went to the cinema, dancing. England, Argentina, Falklands, Malvinas . . . we came from opposite sides of the war but it was a beautiful love story. Then suddenly he was sent to the Falklands and it was over. Then he returned to England and we kept in contact by phone and plenty of letters and cards. A few years passed and we lost contact.

'I suppose he could be married now, I'm married too. It is very important to me to contact him, I don't want to bother him, only that he meant a lot to me and maybe there were some misunderstandings due to distance and difference of age, but I still remember him. Now I'm forty-three and I see things more clear . . . ' Two days after the item appeared, a message arrived from Andrea: 'Michael's sister told him about your story in the newspaper. He contacted me by e-mail and we chatted on the instant messenger. He even showed me on the webcam your Missing article, with his photo. I can't express how thankful I am with you, I'll never forget this.'

12

1 August 2009

In June we featured an item on Ron Hooker's search for his old mate and fellow beefcake, Maurice Arthur, with whom he served in the Royal Marines a half-century ago. His photo shows the pair of them in 1958 when they were at the RM Infantry

Beefcakes Maurice and Ron, 1958

Training Centre at Lympstone, Devon, posing before going for a swim in the River Exe. Ron informed us: 'After training I joined 40 RM Commando and Maurice went to 45 Commando. He was a talented tenor who played the part of the solo singing soldier in the film *Oh What a Lovely War*, and sang with the George Mitchell Choir and the *Black and White Minstrel Show*.'

Success! An e-mail came from Carol Davis, Maurice's long-term friend and carer: 'We've been living in Burry Port, Carmarthenshire, for the past three years,' she wrote, 'having moved here from north London. Maurice is long retired from his singing career and has suffered some ill health, but carries on regardless. He'd love to hear from Ron. That photo was a real surprise and caused quite a lot of mirth!'

We also reconnected Maurice with a delighted Harry Sharples, the friend he shared a London flat with in the seventies. They'd met as fellow singers with Glyndebourne Opera in Sussex. 'Maurice often talked about his days in the Marines and what great buddies he had there. The one toothbrush they shared while on desert ops, the electric razor he had which shaved the whole troop, the scrapes they got into. He was a great gymnast and he and I used to go running together and do weight training. I'd play the piano and we'd sing together. He was also well known in theatrical circles, counting quite a few famous actors as his friends. A lot turned up at his parties, as well as some East End villains, which made for some intense events!'

13

9 May 2009

In February we published an item on Paul Brooker's search for descendants of the notables on an old photo of Britain's early aviation pioneers, taken on 4 May 1909. He informed us of the centenary celebration of the Birth of British Aviation to be held this very weekend, as it was exactly one hundred years ago that the first flight in this country by a British pilot took place. The pilot was the dashing twenty-five-year-old J. T. C. Moore-Brabazon – later Lord Brabazon of Tara – and he entered the history books by flying his 50hp Voisin bi-plane, the Bird of Passage, 500 yards at a height of about 50ft.

Aviation pioneers on the Isle of Sheppey in 1909

Among those shown on the photo are the Short Brothers (who set up the world's first aircraft factory), pioneer flyer Charles Rolls (of Rolls Royce fame), and Wilbur and Orville Wright – the world's first successful aviators. They are pictured before the doorway of the Mussel Manor Aero Clubhouse at Shellbeach on the Isle of Sheppey. Paul wrote: 'I'm a bank manager and aviation enthusiast, and I'm organising the celebration together with Sharon and Terry Munns, owners of Mussel Manor – now a holiday park called Muswell Manor. I hope to take a photo exactly a hundred years later with descendants of those shown standing outside the same doorway.'

Happily, as a result of this column, the present Lord Brabazon, the brilliant aviator's grandson, is joined today on Sheppey by descendants of Messrs Short Brothers: Oswald, Horace and Eustace. They are Deborah Mackay, whose great-grandfather was the Short brothers' cousin, and the brothers' grand-niece, Elizabeth Walker. They will be enjoying a fly-past of vintage planes from the Second World War, live entertainment and a good old-fashioned nosh-up.

14

31 January 2009

In December we reported that we'd managed to locate a couple of Sue Powell and Ann Parrott's erstwhile colleagues from the sixties. They worked for Associated British Cinemas (later taken over by EMI) in Golden Square, London, dealing with the accounts for ABC cinemas nationwide.

'There was great camaraderie,' recalled Sue. 'We saw each other

ABC ladies in London in the Swinging Sixties

through heartbreaks of unrequited love and went to discos and dance halls together, often returning home on the milk train. Over the years Ann and I have lost touch with most of them. But we'd love to find them and hold a reunion.'

Well, we've netted another fine crop of ABC workmates. Janice Silver-Magnus writes: 'Your column brought back memories of my happy times at ABC, working for Mr McDonald, the Financial Director, in 1965–7. It was an exciting place, as you never knew which famous person might pop in. My boss was very kind, letting me watch films in the screening room if we weren't too busy.'

Jeanne Barr says: 'I was so pleased to read today's Missing and Found. I worked for ABC between 1947 and 1950. I always read your column but never thought I'd see anything that referred to me.' We heard from Suzanne Rummery, ABC employee in

1962–9, now living in Berkshire. And this from Brian Santilli, who started at ABC as a post boy in 1960 before being promoted to the staff restaurant as a commis chef: 'I still remember the day Cliff Richard lunched there and sent me his compliments for my steamed sponge pudding.' Ah, heady days!

15

15 November 2008

Way back in June of last year Ernst Katz from Siegen in Germany recalled his cycling tour of Holland in the summer of 1958, when he was a young man of twenty-one. He stayed in a youth hostel in Amsterdam, full of guests who slept in crowded dormitories and had breakfast together. 'We were enthusiastic about international friendships and I met an English student there, Denis Hardy, who was also travelling through Holland, mostly by hitch-hiking,' wrote Ernst.

Ernst as land surveying student in 1958

'He was likeable and clever. We went sightseeing together and discussed politics, girls, our studies and plans for the future. He studied to be a doctor in London. When parting we promised to write to each other. Indeed, there was a short communication. Then we lost touch. When visiting London in 2006 I remembered those sunny days long ago. I would like to know where Denis lives and whether he remembers his mate Ernst, who is a retired land-surveyor today.'

Quite why it's taken so long I've no idea, but Denis just e-mailed to say he had been sent the clipping and was astonished to learn that Ernst was looking for him. He was keen to make contact. 'I am a paediatrician,' he tells us, 'at present working at the Royal Hospital, Sharjah, and living in Dubai. I'm married with three children and about to be a grandfather. Luckily I'm in good health, do a lot of sports and have run in four marathons. I've written many medical articles and intend to try my hand at novels – probably after I retire in three years' time. Many thanks for reuniting me with an old friend from my youth.'

16

11 October 2008

In June we published an item on Peter Street, who was looking for former members of the Domino Road Club, a cycling club from Manchester in the early fifties. The club was affiliated to the British League of Racing Cyclists and dedicated to promoting massed-start racing on the open roads. It won more than two hundred races throughout the fifties and sixties and its members included four national champions and many regional champions, as well as winners of races in the Isle of Man International Cycling Week.

In August we managed to reconnect Peter with a long-lost chum and former colleague, George Booth. The pair worked together at C. Nicholls, a printing company in Manchester. And

Peter Street and fellow cyclists of the Domino Road Club in 1954

although George was not a member of the Domino Road Club, he was a cyclist, too – a member of the Manchester Clarion, one of Britain's oldest cycling clubs.

Now, finally, we have heard from one of Peter's erstwhile Domino Road cyclists – Peter Blease of St Mary Bourne, Hampshire. 'I was very surprised to see myself in the photograph taken fifty-four years ago, which appeared in your column,' he e-mailed. 'I am the one in the middle, with Peter Street on the right, and Roger Morris (I think that was his name) on the left. Behind me is Albert Hope, who rode with the senior section of the club. We were all junior members at the time. I would be very happy if you could pass on my contact details to Peter Street.'

17

27 September 2008

Last month Clive Taylor of Lincolnshire was searching for the missing members of his historic five-man Vulcan bomber crew. They belonged to 617 Squadron and on 20–21 June, 1961, flew in Vulcan (B1A) XH 481 on the first ever non-stop flight from the UK to Australia. They flew from Scampton, near Lincoln, to Richmond, near Sydney in 20 hours, 3 minutes and 17 seconds from take-off to landing, re-fuelling in flight three times on the way. Afterwards, the men flew together for a long

Vulcan bomber crew, 1961

while as a top-rated Bomber Command crew before going their separate ways.

Clive had recently met up with the crew's captain Mike Beavis – who was knighted and retired from the RAF as Air Chief Marshall – and they hoped to track down the remaining three crew members: John Knight (Air Electronics Officer), Dave Bromley (Co-Pilot) and Geoff Jukes (Navigator Plotter).

John Knight's son Andrew wrote to tell us that sadly his father died in 1999. But an e-mail also arrived from Dave Bromley, very much alive and well: 'Firstly I must thank you for your column. It brought back fond memories of my time in the RAF. Flying the Vulcan bomber was the most enjoyable and rewarding experience of my working life. After working as a co-pilot for a year, I completed the captain's course and served a further four years in that role. On leaving the RAF I worked in the civil service and am now retired and living in Southport, devoting my energies to the more leisurely pursuits of golf and bowls. I'm very much looking forward to meeting up with my old crew again.'

18

6 September 2008

In July we featured the tale of John Smith of Dover, who was searching for old comrades with whom he served on the Hospital Ship El Nil, converted from King Farouk's royal barge. John was on board for eighteen months in the late forties as a member of the Royal Army Medical Corps.

'Most of these men are now in their eighties,' said John, 'and I'll be eighty myself next birthday. In the photo I am fifth from the

Crew of El Nil hospital ship in 1947

right, second row down. We were attached to Netley Hospital, Southampton, and sailed through the Mediterranean and the Suez Canal down to Mombasa in Kenya, where we picked up British troops left over from the war. Our next port of call was Aden, then Port Said, Malta, Tobruk, Benghazi, Gibraltar and so back home to Southampton. I hope you can reunite me with my old shipmates.'

Sidney Wheeler-Bailey wrote: 'I was a crew member in 1945–6, during which time we called at Bombay and Mombasa and gave a sea burial to six Italian ex-POWs in the Red Sea. Then we sailed through the Suez Canal and on to Naples for discharge. I had a tooth extracted by the RAMC and a charming sister held my hand during the painful process.'

Alan Thompson responded: 'I, too, served on this ship, joining at Southampton in December 1947 *en route* to India. I have the photo in front of me now and remember quite a few of the lads.' And Peter McCready added: 'I was not a member of the crew, but sailed home from Port Said on the *El Nil* as a patient in

1947. I was bedbound and saw few of the crew, but the care I received was wonderful.'

John has now heard from a total of ten El Nil contacts. 'This has turned out far better than I expected. A Great Big THANK YOU.'

19

12 July 2008

Joan Herbertson in her youth

Here's an unusual one, dear readers. For the first time in the nine (yes, nine!) years that I've been writing this popular little column, I've been credited with unearthing a 'missing' person through my *karma* alone. Most gratifying!

To explain, Tony Wright had asked me to track down his long-lost cousin Joan Herbertson, née Elliott, the daughter of Tony's father's sister Minnie Wright, who married Tommy Elliott and lived in Morpeth in Northumberland until their deaths many years ago. Still with me?

Tony's father, Thomas Wright, was lost at sea when the SS *Empire Mica* was sunk by torpedoes off the coast of Florida in June 1942. He was thirty-two and Tony was just five – a few years younger than Joan. Contact with her was lost years ago, but

Tony wanted to find her for the sixty-sixth anniversary of his father's death, to be marked by a family visit to the wreck of the *Empire Mica* and by placing a plaque in the lighthouse overlooking the cape where it sank.

Alas, I couldn't take his story on, due to the large volume of requests I receive. Sadly, I can't publish them all. But I e-mailed Tony encouragingly, with much information on other avenues to pursue, and urged him not to abandon his search. He wrote back: 'I had tried so many other ways to get in touch with her, but no sooner had you sent me your e-mail than there I was speaking on the phone to Joan at her new home in Darlington! This was as a result of an earlier inquiry I had made, but you provided me with a way to keep hoping which was justified in the end. This must be one of your quickest results in locating a lost relative. I put it down to the impact you had.'

20

21 June 2008

Earlier this year we featured an item about former 'trolley dolly' Diana Gray, who we reunited with some of the other stewardesses she worked with at Monarch Airlines when it was launched in April 1968. The airline celebrated the fortieth anniversary of its first revenue flight in April and our photo shows the airline's first sixteen stewardesses, with Diana second from the right.

One of the erstwhile stewardesses we found was Jean Jones, née Smith, who tells us: 'My mother-in-law saw the item in your column and phoned me late at night, with mug of cocoa in hand, to tell me about it. She always does the crossword puzzle in the

Monarch stewardesses on 5 April 1968,
Diana Gray is second from right

Mail, God bless her, so it caught her eye. We original Monarch girls were the prototype hostesses and were looked after very well. In those days you had to have something special to make the grade. I'm now an actress and photographer and live in Salisbury, Wiltshire.'

After running the follow-up item, we received a further interesting e-mail from Mary-Anne Hardie, daughter of the founder of Monarch Airlines, Bill Hodgson. Mary-Anne's mother designed the stewardesses' uniforms. 'Monarch was very much a family firm to start with,' she writes, 'and even *I* played a part in its foundation. Although I was only nine at the time I wanted to call it Vulture Airways! I was privileged to see the first Britannia take off from Luton Airport in 1968, and used to go up to Luton as a great treat during my holidays. As a teenager I worked in the firm's accounts department.

'Sadly my parents are now both dead, but it's been lovely for me to revisit a few memories of the family firm which started with only two Britannias and a contract signed on our dining room table, which we still refer to as the "Monarch table".'

We put Mary-Ann in touch with Diana. 'What a lovely surprise to get an e-mail from such an important person. Many thanks for forwarding it on to me – it's now gone to thirty other people, including some in Australia.'

21

14 June 2008

In this column in April Jacki Adcock of Leicester was looking for a man she dated back in 1959–60, the then pop singer Danny Hunter, whose real name was Johnny Goossens. They met on the Isle of Wight, where Jacki was working as a waitress and Danny was singing at the Copacabana Club. 'I remember Danny had been in the Merchant Navy on the MS *Mauretania*,' recalled Jacki, 'together with Tommy Steele, before he became famous. Amazingly, Tommy visited the Copacabana while we were on the Isle of Wight and they met up again then. It was a memorable evening for all who were there.'

Danny and Jacki when they were stepping out together, 1959

They dated through the summer of 1959, then went

their separate ways. But they met again the following year when Danny played a gig at De Montfort Hall in Jacki's home-town of Leicester, sharing a bill with the Everly Brothers. Jacki recalled that the date was 17 April, the same day that Eddie Cochran died and that Danny, who knew him, was very upset by the tragic news. They lost touch after that.

A delighted Danny, aka Johnny, saw the item and contacted us. We gave Jacki his phone number and she e-mailed to update us: 'Thanks so much for putting me in touch with Danny. What an amazingly quick response! We've had several chats on the phone and enjoyed going over our shared memories, as well as catching up on the past forty-nine years. Danny told me that after we parted he signed a recording contract with HMV and made several successful records. Then he toured the US and Europe, rubbing shoulders with famous names in the rock and pop world of the sixties. Eventually he settled down to life here with his family and is now enjoying a happy semi-retirement in a lovely East Sussex village. He doesn't perform in public any more, but still loves his music and song-writing. We're looking forward to meeting up later this summer.'

22

31 May 2008

A big response to last month's item regarding Michael Norris and his search for Old Boys of the London Choir School in Kent, which closed fifty years ago. Founded in the Twenties, the LCS provided choirs for many famous London churches, as well as choral soundtracks for films. The LCS went on three tours of

London Choir School boys going on tour in 1930

North America before the Second World War and one of its most gifted sopranos, Iwan Davies, appeared before King George V in 1932. Michael (a pupil at the school from 1948 to 1954) is compiling an anthology of the Old Boys' recollections.

One of the many who e-mailed in response was Alwyn Longford. 'My Sunday church was Christ Church, Lancaster Gate,' he wrote, 'but I sang at many others. I appeared in the Laurence Olivier film Henry V and in a photograph on a Christmas card designed for American soldiers to send home – this photo also appeared on the cover of *Picture Post* magazine. I'll be pleased to help in any way I can.'

Eric Shorter wrote: 'My step-brother Kenneth attended the school and his voice is on the soundtrack of the 1939 weepie *Goodbye Mr Chips*, starring Robert Donat. He also sang at the Royal Albert Hall. His daughter has his old school reports. Family history has it that when his (and my) father could no longer afford the school fees, the school kept him on without charge, so good was his voice.'

Neil Hamilton, who joined the school in 1955, recalls singing at Stirling Moss's wedding, being on TV for a Christmas special and performing at St Paul's Cathedral. Other Old Boys who e-mailed included Geoff Couzens, Neville Wilkie and Ivor Foster, with tales galore.

23

3 May 2008

Dear readers, you'll doubtless recall our item from January about Sylvia Young OBE – she of the renowned Sylvia Young Theatre School in London, alma mater of Amy Winehouse, Billie Piper and Denise van Outen – who was looking for an old friend called Judy Samuels. Sylvia was last in touch with Judy thirty-five years ago, when they were due to have lunch together – in Grimsby, of all places – but due to a bizarre misunderstanding the meeting never took place.

It was all to do with Sylvia – who was then holidaying up North – being urgently called back to London for work purposes, and being unable to reach Judy to let her know. Ah, those distant days before mobile phones! Due to Sylvia's embarrassment over the fiasco she never called Judy after that, although she did eventually write to her, only to find that Judy had moved, so the letter never reached her. The unfortunate episode had been on Sylvia's conscience ever since and she wanted at long last to apologise, as she felt her old friend must still be mystified by it all.

An e-mail arrived from Judy: 'I've just returned from a trip abroad to find several messages in my in-box telling me about an article relating to me that appeared in the *Daily Mail*. If I am the

Sylvia Young, on the left, in the sixties

Judy Samuels that Sylvia is looking for, I'd be delighted to catch up with her!' So, far from the Grimsby mix-up preying on her mind for the past thirty-five years, she didn't even remember it. Still, the two friends are back together now and can clear up any lingering misunderstandings.

24

12 April 2008

No doubt you all recall our story from last November about Brian Harper's search for Doreen Ash, a Second World War child evacuee to Donyatt, a small Somerset village between Chard and Ilminster. As part of a heritage project, the village intends to rebuild the old railway halt – abandoned in 1962 – to which the evacuees arrived on 3 September 1939.

Brian had in his possession an old letter from Doreen's mother containing instructions for whoever took in her five-year-old daughter. 'If I send my little girl pocket money, will you give her a penny a day?' she wrote touchingly. A childless couple took in Doreen and apparently she was very happy with them. 'We plan to make a life-sized sculpture of Doreen, complete with a small suitcase, and set it on the platform beside the station name,' wrote Brian. 'In the small waiting hut we will tell her story and show pictures dating from that period.'

Doreen Ash as a child

Lo and behold a letter duly arrived from Doreen, now seventy-five-year-old Mrs Grinham of Ashford, Kent, a grandmother of five. I e-mailed Brian and he wrote back: 'Within a minute of receiving your news I was speaking to an excited Doreen and hearing wonderful stories of her time in Donyatt. If we are successful in our lottery grant a seven-year-old Doreen will appear as a bronze statue on our new station halt, and she will be guest of honour at our opening ceremony.' Come on you lottery people – cough up.

25

22 March 2008

We recently featured David McCarthy's search for former British soldiers who had served at the Atlit army camp on the Mediterranean coast near Haifa, built by the British during our Mandate in Palestine. It was used as a detention camp for Jewish refugees from the Holocaust who tried to enter Israel illegally.

The camp operated from 1939 to 1948, when the Mandate ended and the State of Israel was born. It's now a museum commemorating this tragic episode when thousands of Jews arrived by sea on creaking old ships. Our navy mounted a blockade to prevent the ships from docking. But some ran the blockade, only to be stopped and escorted into Haifa, from where the refugees were taken to Atlit.

The museum asked for reminiscences from British guards at Atlit, and we were able to provide plenty: from Cyril King (then a twenty-one-year-old Royal Artillery gunner charged with guarding the notorious Stern Gang), John Owen, Pat Briggs, and also from Arthur Partridge of the Royal Horse Artillery, who escorted refugees off the ships to the barbed-wire enclosed camp. 'It was a pitiful sight,'

Atlit army camp, Palestine

Arthur recalled. 'I didn't envy the chaps who had to squirt DDT Powder, used to stop the spread of diseases, inside the refugees' clothing as they stood in long queues.'

Now we've heard from Fiona Molloy, daughter of John O'Dea, who was in the same regiment as Arthur Partridge and is pictured with him in the photo Arthur sent us. 'I cannot describe my father's delight in reading the item,' says Fiona. 'He is most keen to resume contact with Arthur, whom he knew very well. My father met up with him after their demob in 1948, but sadly they lost touch afterwards.' That has now been rectified.

26

8 March 2008

Two months ago we had an item about Dick Waterhouse, who was looking for missing members of his Ancient & Honourable Order of Tibetian Layabouts, a 'mutual admiration society' and the world's most secret jazz club, which this month is holding its 50th annual dinner.

The Order is comprised of jazz aficionados who in the fifties turned up *en masse* at the major jazz events. And once a week they met at the home of Alfred Grove, where the latest jazz LPs were played and discussed over tea and sandwiches. At that time Gladys Grove was collecting funds to help Tibetan orphans and the club members supported her, so she named them her Tibetian (her own eccentric spelling) Girls and Boys. Others, however, regarded the jazz fans as mere layabouts, and hence their name was born.

Good news: we've found five of the original Tibetian Lay-

The Tibetian Layabouts in 1959

abouts, and a far-flung bunch they are. E-mails whizzed in from Ken Jeavons, John and Adele Piddock (now of sunny Spain), Peter Wright (now of *la belle* France) and Linda Sofianos, who writes on behalf of her brother, now residing in Bermuda. Linda tells us: 'I've tried for the past twenty years to trace the Layabouts for him, but without success.' My dear, you should have come to us.

So it's gearing up for a cracking reunion this month. Bring on the tea and sandwiches, and put on the George Melly records.

23 February 2008

*Victorian theatre architect
Frank Matcham*

Last December David Cooper wrote asking if we could trace eighty-seven-year-old Peggy Huggins, whose grandfather was Frank Matcham (1854–1920), the distinguished British theatre architect who designed some one hundred and fifty theatres across Britain, including the London Palladium, Victoria Palace Theatre, London Coliseum and Hackney Empire.

David is vice-chairman of the Frank Matcham Society ('dedicated to the appreciation and enjoyment of great theatres everywhere'), and together with English Heritage, the society erected a blue plaque at Matcham's London residence at 10 Haslemere Road in Crouch End, N8. It was unveiled by the society's patrons, married-couple actors Prunella Scales and Timothy West. And although Peggy couldn't be found in time to invite her to the event, David hoped to make her aware of it.

An e-mail arrived from Sue Loch, great-grand-daughter of Frank Matcham, who helpfully put David in touch with Peggy Huggins. 'I do remember Peggy's parents quite well,' she says. 'I sometimes went to visit them when I was a child and they lived in Pinner in north London. I last spoke to Peggy about five years ago.'

So, all being well, Peggy will soon be making a little trip to her grandfather's house in Crouch End, to pay her respects to the great architect – surely a moving moment in her twilight years.

28

25 August 2007

Last month we published the story of Victor Wright, now living in Connecticut, USA. On 15 February, 1952, he was one of the eight pall-bearers at King George VI's funeral. He told us that he could account for all the pall-bearers except for one, who was missing – Robert Dilworth. At the time of the funeral, Victor was twenty-one and a member of the King's Company, Grenadier Guards, as were all the other pall-bearers. They were all later awarded the Royal Victorian Medal by the late Queen Mother.

Sadly, we heard from Robert Dilworth jnr that his father passed away in 1998. But a number of other e-mails have whizzed in, regarding some of Victor's erstwhile friends in the Grenadier Guards, who were also involved in the historic funeral. Tug Wilson and Jeff Baker, for example, were bearskin carriers. In other words, they carried the pall-bearers' bearskins while the bearers were carrying the coffin. 'I can still picture Tug straddling his bed, playing an imaginary trombone,' mused Victor from across the Atlantic.

And then there is C. P. Snook, whose nephew contacted us. Snook was batman to CSM Freddie Clutton, the man who

Pall-bearers carrying the coffin at George VI's funeral, 1952

walked directly in front of the coffin. 'After the funeral I never returned to public duties and lived outside of barracks,' said Victor. 'And I was demobbed in 1953, right after the Coronation, so I lost touch with my buddies.' We hope he and some of his old buddies will be back in touch now.

29

11 August 2007

Glamorous one-time model Barbara Fairs, née Craig, contacted us in June to see if we could find her friend and former flatmate Dory Swan from the fifties. Dory, originally from Tyneside, was a small-time actress and model, who was featured on the cover *Reveille* magazine in a bikini, and did TV and other advertising. 'She did a great advert for English Rose Underwear which was on billboards all over London,' Barbara recalled.

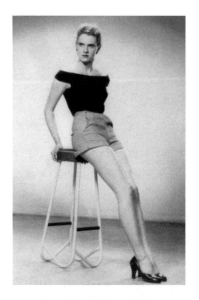

Pretty blonde Dory later lived with famous water speed ace Donald Campbell for two years in Dolphin Square, London. ('I stayed with her there once whilst Donald was away in Australia,' wrote Barbara.) But that relationship ended abruptly when Donald

Model Barbara Craig in the fifties

fell for the singer Tonia Bern, who he went on to marry in 1958. Barbara last saw Dory in 1959, when she was doing a fashion show for an underwear firm in Newcastle. Dory afterwards moved to New York. And years later she was mentioned in Tonia Bern-Campbell's memoir of her husband, *My Speed King*.

Well, there's good news and bad news. The good: Barbara and her old friend have now been reunited and Barbara e-mailed to thank us: 'Dory is still living in New York. She's been quite a girl and had a very interesting life, mixing in wealthy circles. I hope to go and see her sometime within the next few months.' The bad: 'Alas, she's not in good health, has had a stroke and has ended up with very little.'

30

3 February 2007

At the end of last year Anthony Holroyd of Elland, West Yorkshire, wrote about his intriguing visit to Yugoslavia in August 1953 as part of a group of twenty British children whose fathers were killed there during the Second World War. They had been invited by President Tito himself. Anthony celebrated his 15th birthday during the visit.

The youngsters saw their fathers' graves in the British Military Cemetery in Belgrade, then travelled to the island of Brioni, where they lunched with Tito at his holiday villa, had their photos taken and got his autograph. Afterwards they took Tito's private train to Zagreb, from where they transferred to Dubrovnik and then to Crikvenica, on the Adriatic, for a further fortnight before returning home.

Anthony Holroyd (at rear, in the middle behind the two girls) and the other children with Tito in 1953

Anthony hoped to find others from this memorable trip, and in this we succeeded. We heard from Frederick Smith, the stepfather of Jane and Susan Royle, who were also on the visit. Says Frederick: 'Their father, Frank Royle, was part of 42 Royal Marine Commando, which was completely wiped out. Jane remembers Anthony and has a copy of the same photo you showed in the paper. She's married and lives in Spain. Susan is also married and lives in Australia.'

And John Wardman Holmes wrote: 'My sister Marie and I are on the photo, standing on either side of the President. We were the only children from Wales in the group, and had been invited because our father was killed when his Halifax bomber crashed in the mountains whilst on a mission to drop supplies to Tito's partisans.'

31

6 January 2007

Excellent news regarding our search for former German POW Heinz Bottger, imprisoned at POW Camp 801 on Guernsey during the Second World War. Readers might recall that Heinz was befriended by Englishman Stanley Lamb, a guard at the camp. As the official camp translator, Heinz tried to teach Stanley German – not altogether successfully.

The two friends from opposite sides of the war corresponded for a while after Stanley was demobbed and moved to Chester-le-Street, County Durham. In the last letter Stanley got from Heinz, then in a POW camp in Oxfordshire, he wrote 'I am still a bit afraid of what to do when I come home as it will not be possible for me to continue in the merchant navy. I am considering to

German soldier Heinz Bottger

leave Germany and try to find a job abroad in a country where conditions of life are better than in our war threatened Europe. It is a pity Stan, but you see how difficult it is for the different governments to agree on the smallest questions.' (So no change there, then.) Unfortunately Stanley lost track of Heinz in 1946 and never knew whether he returned to his home-town of Hamburg, or settled elsewhere.

Now we have the answer. Stanley's daughter Eve Stocks e-mailed to announce: 'We've found him, and it's all thanks to you! He's well and living in Hamburg and was thrilled to be back in touch with Dad. They spoke on the phone and have arranged to meet up. Heinz is due to visit Newcastle in May, but that's a long time away when you're in your eighties, so I'll see if I can get them together sooner. We're all very excited.'

Heinz was found via a circuitous route. A reader who saw the item knew of a German POW called Heinz Bottger, but it was mere coincidence – he turned out to be the wrong one. Nevertheless, that Heinz's widow put Stanley in touch with an organisation in Hamburg which traces German wartime personnel, and they found our Heinz within a week. So it's Schnappses all 'round!

32

23 December 2006

Last month we featured an item about Dan Benjamin of Edgware,
north London, who with his partner Colin Wild ran the Carnaby
Cavern, a famous boutique off London's Carnaby Street, from
1965 to 1978. They had many famous customers, including
Benny Hill, Jimi Hendrix, Shirley Bassey, Bob Hoskins and the
pop group Status Quo.

'The Quo, in their autobiography XS All Areas, refer to the
Carnaby Cavern as the most fashionable store in the world!' Dan
declared. Feeling nostalgic for his days at the cutting edge of
Swinging Sixties' fashion, he was eager to trace some of the
memorable characters who worked for them and came over all

Dan Benjamin with wife Brenda in 1976

lyrical. 'We know all about the famous folk, our interest is in our friends, the staff. Like those brilliant tailors – Otis, the very best, (remember the leather catsuits he made for Alvin Stardust?) and our very first tailor, Stephano, and Roger, who made the jackets for *Hi-de-Hi*, they had to be badly made, as jackets were in the forties . . . and Phillip, who taught me to cut . . . so many memories, so many stories.'

We heard straight away from one of Dan's ex-employees, John Banyard. He tells us his story: 'Before Danny had Carnaby Cavern, he had a men's clothes shop in Windsor Street, Uxbridge, called Michael Martin, the names of his two sons. I started working for Danny and Colin as a schoolboy in 1964. I was about thirteen at the time. I used to ride to Uxbridge on my bike after school and on Saturdays to take clothes to be altered to a Mrs Chambers in Montague Road. She used to make shirts with enormous collars for the bands Deep Purple and Sweet. I also did things like making tea, sweeping up, etc. Later I worked at the Carnaby Cavern. I remember being there one Saturday when Colin threw fireworks up and down the street to try and lure people into the shop. I remember Levi jeans were £2 12*s* 6*d* at the time. I left in 1968. I now live in Jersey and wish Danny well.'

33

9 December 2006

John Harrison (left) in Korea

Two months ago I wrote about John Harrison of Ripley, Derbyshire, who was searching for the National Service comrades with whom he served in Korea in 1953–4. He was in the Signal Platoon of the Royal Warwickshire Regiment. In the summer of 1953 he sailed on the *Empire Orwell* from Southampton to Pusan, Korea. His battalion joined the 28th Brigade 1st Commonwealth Division replacing the Durham Light Infantry.

'We were the first battalion to land after the ceasefire and were camped on the 38th Parallel,' he wrote, 'patrolling up to the Pintail Bridge on the River Imjin. My time was spent in the Signal Office, as I was the NCO in charge of telephone exchange, control wireless battalion network, despatch riders and all official mail in and out of the battalion. The atmosphere was tense, because we all expected the war to start up again by Christmas, and we had many air raids and stand-to procedures to keep us on our toes. There was a lot of pressure on us, and on Christmas Eve a young second lieutenant – I remember he was from Grimsby – shot himself because he couldn't take it any more.'

Many letters arrived from John's erstwhile Korean War

comrades, including P. Whitworth, E. Lightfoot, and Denis Woods. Tom Ewart, who served with the Royal Scots Rand and now lives in Dumfries, says: 'I sailed from Southampton on 5 June 1953 aboard the *Empire Fowey* and arrived in Pusan on 7 July. I spent the next year based on the 38th Parallel between the Teal and Pintail bridges. I'd love to hear from John and meet him.'

John writes: 'The response we've had was beyond my wildest dreams. Many thanks and more successes with your column.'

34

9 September 2006

In 1966 Neil Kennedy travelled overland with three friends – John Savidge, Tony Long and John Humphreys – to Pakistan via Iran and Afghanistan, returning via Iraq and other exotic Middle Eastern ports of call. They came back leaner and fitter and had enjoyed it so much that they resolved to undertake another great motoring journey – from London to Cape Town. 'Employment had to be obtained to finance this grand plan,' Neil explained, ' so I set myself a target of £150 and started work as an ice-cream salesman on the day that England won the World Cup.' A few months later, with the adventurers' number having swelled to twelve, they set off.

The following year Neil and his travelling companions returned home and sadly lost contact. But thanks to our good offices, the original 'gang of four' have been reunited and are meeting up in Cape Town next year.

Neil recalls the distant adventure: 'After travelling through wet

*Neil (2nd from right) and friends leave London for overland
trip to Cape Town, 1966*

and cold France and Spain, the warmth of Morocco was most
welcome, especially as two of our jeeps had, because of the strong
winds, lost their canvas tops. We drove along the coast to Algiers,
which showed the scars of its recent war of independence. Here
we prepared for the Sahara by taking on extra water and fuel,
then travelled through Algeria, Niger and down to Lagos in
Nigeria, where we sold one of the jeeps, as we didn't have the
funds for all three to continue.

'After two weeks of beach life in Lagos, we boarded the SS *Ilorin
Palm* for Luanda in Angola, which was then a Portuguese colony
with guerrilla war problems. We made it down through the dense
bush into South West Africa, now called Namibia. More bush and
many rivers later we rolled into Cape Town on 2 February, 1967,
with 124 days and over 9000 miles behind us . . . '

35

2 September 2006

In July we published a story about Roy 'Chick' Edwards of Bexley, Kent, who was looking for his former fellow scouts from the 11th Dartford Troop. 'I was fortunate to have been leader of this group of well-disciplined lads in the late fifties and throughout the Sixties,' said Roy. 'It was a time when scouts still wore shorts, when they could play rough games without living in fear of the health and safety authorities, and when scouters weren't taken to court if a lad had a minor accident.'

He recalled the Troop's 'fantastic *esprit de corps*' and was proud of the fact that between 1962 and 1968 it produced twenty-four

11th Dartford Scout Troop at a jamboree in 1961, with Roy Edwards standing on extreme left

Queen's Scouts – the highest honour to which a scout can aspire, requiring top standards in skills such as first aid, firefighting and public health, and the ability to survive outdoors in all weathers.

One of the scouts Roy sought was Steve Rackstraw (aka Racky), who e-mailed to say that a relative had sent him the item. Steve, who now lives in Mexico, wrote: 'I'd love to contact Chick and thank him for the many happy hours I enjoyed in his scout group. Thanks to him I learned a great deal which stood me in excellent stead later in life. I've been an incurable traveller and have had many adventures around the world, for which my scout training was a great preparation. Thank you for facilitating the chance for me to express my gratitude.'

It's a pleasure.

36

22 July 2006

Happy news for Gordon Murrell regarding his long-lost brother Charles. We've gone and found him. Careful followers of this column will recall that last month we featured a plea from Mrs Violet Murrell of Billingshurst in West Sussex, to trace her husband Gordon's elder brother Charles, Best Man at her and Gordon's wedding in 1946. They had lost contact many years ago.

Charles had been in the Territorial Army as a teenager, and was conscripted when the Second World War broke out. Gordon was called up 1942 and sent abroad to Africa. He was later involved in the invasion of Sicily, and was able to meet up with Charles for a short spell in the Italian town of Bari. After the war

Charles (left) and Gordon Murrell, at Gordon's 1946 wedding

Charles married his wife Mary, and they lived in Barnes, south London, while Gordon and his wife lived a little further north in Shepherd's Bush. Then gradually, somehow or other, the brothers went their separate ways. Stuff happens, as someone once said (who was it?). They had five other brothers and sisters, but Gordon lost touch with them all. Families, eh!

The item brought forth a letter from Charles's daughter, Ann Hall, telling us that her father lives with her in Bournemouth, and that he would be thrilled to see Gordon again. The brothers are now a bit on the elderly side, but better late than never. Then another letter arrived, from another long-lost brother – Arthur, who lives in Kingston, Surrey. He's equally keen for a reunion, siblings-wise. Well, the more Murrells the merrier...

37

27 May 2006

Well, it's taken a whole year, but we are pleased to announce that Neil Foster has finally been reunited with the singer of the rock 'n' roll group he belonged to in the sixties. We wrote about his search way back in May 2005, but he's not complaining.

John Day was the lead singer, lead guitarist and van driver of the Delacardoes, one of the few Merseyside bands to feature a tenor saxophonist – namely, Neil himself. 'One night in 1961,' Neil writes, 'John called us together and gave us a pep-talk, the gist of which was that Liverpool was a dead-end place and if we wanted to progress, we had to go to London. We believed him

The Delacardoes in 1961. Left to right: Rodney Day, Neil Foster, Charlie Richmond, John Day

and so we gave up our day-jobs and in 1962 headed down the M1 for fame and fortune, just as things were hotting up in "dead-end" Liverpool! Bad timing, or what? By the way, we all thought the Beatles were the worst pop group on Merseyside.' Ouch!

Inevitably, the band split up and Neil last saw John in 1984. But Neil wrote and published a novel, Cradle of Rock, about their good old Delacardoes days and wanted to give John a signed copy before it was too late. Says Neil: 'Thanks for your help in tracing him and his wife Pauline. We had a great reunion. And I feel certain that although we found each other through an internet search rather than the item in your column, it was nevertheless the *Mail* which started the "ripples on a pond" effect which brought us together again.'

I like that idea. We shall carry on rippling.

38

20 May 2006

A final outing for our successful saga of reunions between former members of the famed Ovaltineys children's radio and stage show from the thirties, involving that talented bunch of performing youngsters who once did so much for the sales of Ovaltine.

Readers might recall the initial request back in January from ex-Ovaltiney twins Fred and Alf Cooper – now living in happy retirement in Luton, Bedfordshire – which led to a reunion with their erstwhile colleague Patricia Lee of Devon. 'How lovely to read about the Cooper twins after all this time,' she wrote. 'I was in the Ovaltineys, too, and even advertised them one year at the Ideal Home Exhibition. Later, in 1952, I appeared in a show

*Alf (left) and Fred (right) with fellow Ovaltiney Desmond
in the middle, in the Thirties*

with Fred and Alf called Over To View, in which I was one of the
dancers called the Tele-Belles. My friend Beryl Butler and I shared
digs with the twins. My name then was Patricia Abrahams but I
used the stage name of Patricia Brahms. I'd love to chat to them
about the old days. We had some very good times.'

Now we have found another ex-Ovaltiney, Margaret Kennedy,
whose stage names were Joy Conway and Betty Hickson.
Margaret, who lives in Enfield, north London, has been married
for sixty-one years to Richard Kennedy, a Big Band musician
who played with the famous Ted Heath. In fact Margaret herself
was a singer with the bands after leaving the Ovaltineys in 1939.
She was a soloist with the Carol Gibbons Orchestra, Phil Green
Orchestra and others. What's more, her daughter is the former
actress Cheryl Kennedy, who is now an acting teacher and stage

director. Cheryl, it will be remembered, was in earlier years married to actor Tom Courtenay. Quite a glittery family.

For one last time, then, let's sing that rousing Ovaltiney signature song:

> *We are the Ovaltineys, little girls and boys.*
> *Make your requests, we'll not refuse you.*
> *We are here just to amuse you . . .*

39

13 May 2006

Last month we featured the tale of Blanche Edwards, now eighty-eight, who was a nineteen-year-old bank clerk in the City of London in October 1936, when the famed Battle of Cable Street took place. That was when Oswald Mosley and his Union of British Fascists marched through the East End, to be met by anti-fascist demonstrators determined to stop them. The police arrested many demonstrators, including Blanche, who was un-ceremoniously carted off by three policemen. She still has vivid memories of the event.

A photographer from the *Daily Express* captured the moment of her arrest, and when it was published in the paper the next day, she was promptly sacked. Blanche later took a job as a 'nippy' at a Lyons Corner House, before going abroad to work as a housekeeper. Twice-widowed, she now lives alone in West Sussex. Although she admitted it was a long shot, she hoped we might find the policemen who arrested her seventy years ago. She had forgiven them.

Blanche is arrested – in the photo which appeared in the Daily Express

Laura Lim e-mailed to say her mother Shirley Wells was pretty sure the policeman on the right was her own father, Geoffrey Head, who had apparently been at the demonstration. 'He was thirty-two in 1936 and is no longer with us, but his wife Esther is still alive at ninety-six. I must say the policeman does have my Grandad's large ears.' Then John Sadler told us the same policeman bore a striking likeness to his own late father, a Metropolitan Police constable from 1936 to 1966. 'Sadly, he passed away in 1990 aged seventy-six,' John wrote.

Finally, a letter arrived from ninety-one-year-old Alf Burtman. No policeman, he, but a fellow anti-Mosley demonstrator. Like Blanche, he was arrested and thrown in the nick during the Battle of Cable Street. By chance he lives near Blanche in West Sussex and is keen to meet her. Still proud of his role in that historic event, we hope to get the two jailbirds together to share their memories.

40

29 April 2006

In March we featured the story of Princess Elizabeth Adesunloye of Nigeria, who lives in Lagos. She described herself as 'an addicted reader of the *Daily Mail* newspaper, even though in Nigeria the paper gets here very late'. The princess, who retired from the Nigerian civil service last year aged sixty – 'with a grand send-off party with TV and many items as retirement gifts' – was hoping to be reunited with Elaine Holley, the kind friend with whose family in Poole, Dorset, she spent many happy holidays decades ago.

Back in the late fifties she was a student at St Martin's School in Solihull, and the educational consultancy of Phillips and Randle in London was managing her stay in England. On leaving St Martin's in 1959 she started a secretarial course at St Godric's College in Hampstead, north London. During the summer holidays she was sent to stay with 'this very loving family, the Holleys', who made her feel at home in England. She recalled the happy times they had – swimming and bicycle

Princess Elizabeth with Elaine Holley in the early sixties

riding, playing tennis and going on excursions to the country and seaside.

She returned to Nigeria in 1962 and has not seen the Holleys since. 'I promised to come back and see them but I was caught up in the Western Nigeria riot of 1965. I lost my then British passport and am just grateful to God that I am alive.' She has tried over the years to trace the Holleys, especially Elaine and her brother Brian.

Happily, this column managed to reunite them within a couple of days. First, an e-mail came from Pat Rose, whose aunt was a neighbour of the Holleys in Poole. She remembers Elizabeth very well and still corresponds with Elaine – now Elaine Sachet, who lives near Looe in Cornwall. She sent us Elaine's address. How helpful is that? Then an e-mail from Mary Lewis, who attended St. Martin's School with Elizabeth and was keen to get in touch with her again. Naturally, we obliged.

'May the Lord enrich you with abundant good health,' a delighted princess wrote to me in her latest e-mail.

41

25 March 2006

*Czech refugee Rosemary Lenart
aged sixteen in 1946*

Well, we've never had a Found like this before. Last December Mary Davison e-mailed from Exeter asking for help in locating a long-lost school friend from the Second World War, Rosemary Lenart. 'Rosemary and her sister Helena were two of the 669 Czech children brought to England in 1939 on the Kindertransport set up by Sir Nicholas Winton,' wrote Mary. 'I believe their parents were later sent to a concentration camp, possibly Buchenwald. With amazing luck, the parents survived the war and the family was reunited in Czechoslovakia in about July 1946.

'Rosemary and I (my name was then Mary Kitt) were together at Sidcup & Chislehurst Technical School, Kent, where we became very close friends. For some time after the war we regularly wrote to each other, but then Rosemary's letters stopped and we lost touch. I would dearly love to trace her and see her again.'

Now, as it happens, I know Sir Nicholas very well. In fact he's a family member, being the father of my partner Nick. So I asked him how we might go about finding Rosemary and Helena. By sheer luck, the two sisters are among the handful of those 669 former child refugees with whom he is still in touch. They live in Budapest. So I gave Mary their contact details and before long she e-mailed again: 'I'm so happy and excited and I can't thank you enough. We have sixty years to catch up with. I'll let you know how we get on.'

If only it was always so easy!

42

24 December 2005

A month ago I wrote about retired insurance broker Jack Hansen's story of his wartime childhood. As a three-year-old, he was evacuated with his parents from their home in Kent to Gwbert-on-Sea, near Cardigan in Wales, because Jack's father was sent to work at the Ministry of Defence Explosives Establishment at nearby Aberporth.

A number of scientists were evacuated from various MoD establishments so that their secret work on explosives could be carried out there, away from German bombers. The MoD requisitioned holiday homes along the coast around Aberporth, which included Gwbert, and installed the evacuated families in them for the duration of the war.

'There were five of us children living with our families at Gwbert and we became good friends,' he recalled. 'We played and studied together. Then in 1947 our families were sent back whence they had come and we all lost touch with each other. We would all be in our late sixties now and I'd love to know what happened to the others.'

Wartime evacuees in Wales,
with Jack Hansen second from the right

One of this select group is Alan Blaiden, now a retired assistant bank manager living in Wimbledon, south London. He wrote: 'The article brought back many memories of our time together at Gwbert-on-Sea. I was very young at the time, but I remember all the names of the other evacuated children – even if I can't put faces to them!' Jack and Alan are now in touch again.

43

10 December 2005

A delighted Ken Drake has been successfully reunited with all of his fellow members of the 1st Fitzwilliam College, Cambridge, rowing eight who won their oars in the May Bumping Races of 1955. (For readers unfamiliar with this delightfully English pastime, a bumping race is a rowing race in which the boats chase each other in single file, with each boat attempting to catch or 'bump' the boat in front without being caught by the boat behind) There had been one member missing from Ken's team – John Hankin – and he asked for our help in locating him, so that he could join in the fiftieth anniversary celebrations this year of the merry event.

Fitzwilliam rowing crew in 1955, with John Hankin on far left in back row and Ken Drake 4th from left in same row

The whole crew and one of their coaches met at Cambridge to have their group photograph taken exactly as they did 50 years ago – even sitting in the same places. Then they changed into their rowing gear and took out Fitzwilliam College's first boat, rowing downstream to visit the spots where they made their bumps fifty years ago. The crew's combined ages totalled 640 years and some of them had not rowed since 1955, yet they managed to row down the Cam for five miles on this occasion.

It was a grand way to celebrate their victory's golden jubilee, especially as the septuagenarians had had their fair share of serious illnesses over recent years, including one serious heart attack, two cases of bowel cancer and a terrifying bout of MRSA.

Well done their team – victorious once again.

44

17 September 2005

Two months ago we published an item about Gordon Lang, who was looking for his best pals – Don Read and Ian Maudlin – from Whitley Bay Grammar School, Tyne & Wear, in the early sixties. He described the three of them as 'a bunch of wasters', explaining: 'We failed our A-levels, so we had to re-sit them at Bath Lane Further Education College. Problem was, we got distracted from our studies by old cars, young girls and Newcastle Brown Ale – but not necessarily in that order.

'We drove around in our old bangers and decamped down to the Rendez-Vous Café and the late-lamented Spanish City Funfair on the sea-front to watch the local "wildlife". The photo I send you was taken outside our grammar school. I'm on the far right,

Don is standing next to me and next to him is Ian, with his eyes on the girls as usual. Don's uncle had a coal merchants' yard opposite the school gates, where he let us keep our cars, so we were always messing about there instead of being at our studies. My mother at this time had a cottage in Alston, Cumbria, and we often drove up there together with another six or seven lads and ran amok in the local pubs and at village dances.'

'The Wasters' with (from the right) Gordon, Don, Ian and an un-named pal

They all lost touch a few years later and Gordon, now a retired Bedfordshire dentist – of all unexpected things for such a 'bad boy' – was keen to reunite with the other two. Luckily, an e-mail breezed in from successful businessman Mike Armstrong of Amersham, Bucks, another member of the old Whitley Bay gang, who is still in touch with Don. Mike informs us that Don is now a distinguished psychologist based in Vancouver, Canada, and recently married a lady called Alison.

So a reunion seems on the cards for these sixtysomethings from Whitley Bay – who have turned out to be anything but wasters – with jugs of Newcastle Brown Ale all 'round.

45

10 September 2005

Lale in her heyday

An interesting update on the item we ran in July concerning George Magnus and his late grandmother, the celebrated German *chanteuse* Lale Andersen. He hoped to hear from Second World War veterans with recollections of Lale and the song most closely connected to her, *Lili Marleen*. She had been the first to record it, in 1939, and it was a favourite with both German and British troops during the war. Even Field Marshal Rommel, Desert Fox of the Afrika Korps, was known to hum it. (Note which may interest readers: my mother, Hungarian wartime *chanteuse* Vali Racz, also recorded *Lili Marleen*, in Hungarian, and this was just as much a favourite with Hungarian troops fighting on the Eastern Front.)

Geoffrey Eyles of Newport, Gwent, wrote in with a most poignant tale. Stationed in the Western Desert in 1941–2, he was sent to Tobruk harbour to help ferry wounded soldiers on to a hospital ship. 'On the jetty were about a hundred walking wounded, mainly German POWs,' he recalls, 'patrolled by military police. One of the POWs took out a mouth organ and began to play *Lili Marleen* quietly. The police reached for their guns, suspecting it might be a signal to revolt, but nobody moved. The tune was slowly taken up by the rest of the soldiers, all singing in wonderful harmony, until it sounded like a well-trained choir.

'Their singing rose to a crescendo which echoed across the harbour waters, and when it was over everybody, the guards included, clapped and clapped. It was a very moving experience, perhaps equalling the rendition of Silent Night on Christmas Eve in the trenches of WWI.'

46

20 August 2005

In June we ran the story of Anne Barnsdall of Nottingham, who was wondering what became of her mother's cousin, former film starlet Rosalie Ashley, once married to celebrity hair-dresser 'Teasie-Weasie' Raymond. Rosalie played in the comedy films *The Captain's Table* and *Too Many Crooks*, both made in 1959. She also appeared in the TV series *Crossroads* in 1964 as the character Jane Templeton.

E-mails whizzed in with news of Rosalie, who is now living near Maidenhead, Berkshire. According to Monty Taylor of Henley-on-Thames: 'She is still very pretty. I saw her in Henley yesterday getting out of her Mercedes.' And Elma Wilson wrote: 'I lived in Birmingham during the sixties and had my hair done at Teasie-Weasie's salon there. I saw Rosalie Ashley at one of his wig shows and she was very beautiful. I remember her from when she co-hosted the BBC's Dancing Club with Victor Sylvester.'

Rosalie Ashley as she is today

Then Rosalie herself e-mailed, to say: 'What a surprise to see myself in your column – I didn't know I was missing! Since Teasie-Weasie died in 1992, life has continued to be busy, with charity and theatre work and a hectic social life. Friends often reminisce about my film career. My favourite role was in *Sons and Lovers*, starring Trevor Howard. They were wonderful, glamorous days.' She and Anne are to meet up again soon.

47

2 July 2005

On 23 April we published an item about Frank Searle, the infamous Loch Ness Monster hunter, who had been well-known during the seventies for the many photos he produced purporting to show Nessie frolicking in the water. His former friend and fellow Nessie enthusiast Roland Watson, an Edinburgh software engineer, was hoping we might root him out so that the two might get together for a chin-wag about their distant Loch Ness adventures.

'He lived permanently by the north shore of Loch Ness in various tents and caravans from 1969 to 1983,' Roland told us, 'whereupon he upped tent pegs and left the Loch for good. Since

Frank Searle in the seventies

that day nothing has been heard from him. It was as if he vanished as quickly as a sight of the monster herself! What I know about him is that his first name was probably Edwin and if he were alive today he would be around eighty years old. He was a cockney by birth and may have returned to his roots. He claimed to have been in the paratroopers up until the mid-fifties, before taking up some manager's role in a London fruit business.'

Sadly, this reunion was not to be. We can now report that, by a curious quirk, Frank Searle died a mere month before our item appeared. Andrew Tullis, a film-maker producing a TV documentary about Searle, discovered that the monster-hunter and one-time paratrooper had been living quietly in the Lancashire town of Fleetwood for the past eighteen years. And this was where he died last March, aged eighty-four. Well, at least we can now let readers know what became of this colourful character.

'Searle was loved and loathed in equal measure,' said Tullis, 'but his place in the history of Loch Ness hoaxes is assured.'

48

2 April 2005

Last April we published the story of Grace Wallace, née Jackson, from Poulton-le-Fylde, Lancashire, who was a member of the Women's Land Army during the Second World War, based first at Aberystwyth in Wales and then Warrington, Cheshire.

She had fond recollections of doing her bit for the war effort as an agricultural worker, and had made many good friends amongst the now-celebrated Land Girls, all of them enthused with that wartime spirit of pulling together and digging for victory. Lend a

Land Girls in Warrington, circa 1944.
Grace is on far right in second row

hand on the land – that was their slogan. Grace was hoping to trace some of the girls she knew. 'I have tried in many ways to get in touch with them,' wrote Grace. ' But so far without success. They would now be pensioners and grandmothers. It would be so good to find out how life has treated them, and to talk about the old times we shared.'

We are pleased to report that the item was successful, and Grace is now in touch with a couple of her wartime agricultural colleagues. One of them is Joan Grimshaw, who served with Grace in Warrington. 'It's such a coincidence,' remarked Grace, 'that Joan has a son who has a business just outside Blackpool, near to where I live, and often comes to visit him. I can't believe she's been so close. Very soon now we are planning to meet up. I'm really looking forward to it.'

49

19 March 2005

Last month we ran an item on Alan Heward, of Wallsend, North Tyneside. For sixty years Alan had been trying to find out the fate of his one-time neighbour, Flight Sergeant Henry Bird, who disappeared when his Lancaster was shot down during a bombing raid over Leipzig in October 1943. Nothing was heard from the plane after take-off. Alan was only twelve at the time but had never forgotten Henry – a good and kind friend – and hoped to locate Henry's sister Dorothy.

'Sixty years is a long time,' wrote Alan, 'and I am now seventy-three. But Dorothy will have her brother's log-book and service records, and I intend to record his service in Bomber Command

Wartime airman Henry Bird

so that he will be remembered. I don't think his name is on any local war memorial.'

Alan has now been reunited with Dorothy, who wrote to him from her home in Dorking, Surrey. Together they visited RAF Wyton in Cambridgeshire, where they were given 'VIP treatment'. They saw the wartime hangars where the Lancasters were kept and the Pathfinder Museum, and went into the control tower overlooking the airfield from which Henry took off on his fateful last bombing mission.

'Dorothy had her brother's log-book, so I could follow every stage of his service with Bomber Command. Now his old school and boys' club and the local library all have his full story. I've made sure he won't be forgotten.'

50

29 January 2005

Last December we featured the theatrical tale of Bob Nichol and Bob Shepherd, aka the Two Palmers, a comedy acrobatic act which toured the country's variety theatres in the mid-fifties. They appeared alongside many headline acts of the day, such as Tennessee Ernie Ford, the wonderful Platters singing combo (who can forget their hit The Great Pretender?), and Frank Randle, whose show was called Randle's Scandals and always had a colourful line-up of artistes.

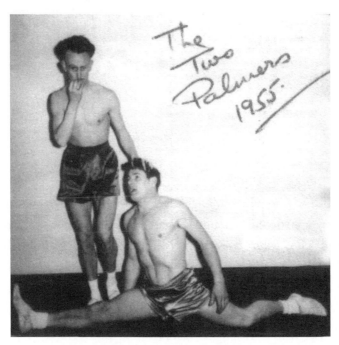

The Two Palmers – Bob Nichol (standing) and
Bob Shepherd – rehearsing in 1955

The Two Palmers (or the two Bobs) loved the theatrical life – travelling around, meeting new people, living in digs with eccentric landladies, the roar of the face paint and the smell of the crowd (ha). But as the variety era fizzled out they went their separate ways and eventually lost touch. Bob Nichol – through his daughter Sheila Bridle, who lives in Cheltenham – contacted this column to see if we might locate his erstwhile stage partner, and I'm glad to say we succeeded.

An e-mail whizzed along from Bob Shepherd, who belongs to the ranks of those lucky Brits who have retired to the sun, in his case to Alicante in Spain (maintaining links with the Old Country via the *Daily Mail*, obviously.) He was only too pleased to be reunited with the other Bob, and the two will no doubt meet up in the near future for much telling of theatrical anecdotes, if perhaps rather less of the acrobatics.

51

1 January 2005

Last month we featured the quirky tale of Harry James of Coventry, who was looking for the lady whom he met and photographed while attending a gathering of a society called the Sealed Knot (don't ask) at Warwick Castle in the summer of 1971. 'It was a three-day event,' he recalled, 'during which participants camped below the Castle in a mock Tudor village, at the centre of which was a large white village cross.

'Early one cool morning, I crawled out of my tent and saw an attractive young woman in a pale blue skirt and white blouse, sitting alone at the base of the cross. Realising it would make a lovely picture, I grabbed my camera and asked whether she would mind having her photo taken. She was very shy but graciously agreed, and I took a couple of shots. I wanted to send her the pictures, so she gave me her address. But I'm ashamed to say I mislaid it before I could ever send them to her.

'I've kept these pictures for the past thirty-three years, hoping one day to be able to give them to her. Her name was Lesley Sammons, and she lived

Lesley Sammons in Harry's 1971 picture

in Leigh-on-Sea, Essex. Of course I tried to locate her, but without any luck. Perhaps your column will have a better chance of tracing her or her family? The photos might bring her back some happy memories of a lovely summer morning many years ago.'

Happily, Lesley e-mailed us in a trice to say her father had called her with the news that her picture was in the paper. 'What a blast from the past!' she exclaimed. 'An incredible surprise and it really made my day. I was eighteen then, now I'm fifty-one.' She and Harry have spoken on the phone and he's sending her the snapshots. Lesley now lives in Hove, Sussex, and is a professional musician with an unusual line of work: she plays piano for opera singers – including some very famous ones such as Kiri Te Kanawa – who are warming up before a live performance.

52

14 August 2004

Scott Angrave had been searching for his one-time best friend Tony King, with whom he lost touch two decades ago. In their youth, the Leicestershire pair were always clowning around and had dreams of becoming professional comedians. They did a few charity gigs and entered one or two competitions in the North and Midlands. They were a great team, Scott told us, and called themselves the Comedy Counts. But at the time, not many would have predicted a career for them in the cut-throat world of showbiz, so they stuck with their day jobs: Tony worked in accountancy and Scott was taking a degree course in business studies.

Then, nineteen years ago, Scott decided to try his luck in America. He upped sticks and headed west with a knapsack on

Comedy Counts – Scott (right) and Tony

his back. And he's been there ever since. He is based in North Carolina and is a successful comedian, performing all over the country. 'It just goes to show that dreams can come true,' he remarked. The last he had heard about his friend Tony, now aged forty-four, was that he had moved to London. But as it turned out, we have found Tony living in their old Leicestershire stamping ground. He is not only in showbiz, but going strong as a successful stand-up and comedy writer. The old friends met up during Scott's recent visit to the UK.

'It was great to see him again,' says Scott. 'He was the one who really started the ball rolling for me in my career. I was finally able to say thank you and catch up with things.'

53

7 August 2004

In June we featured the story of showbiz veteran Rex Graham – stage-named 'Mr Giveaway' – who was trying to trace members of a forties' singing troupe called Steffani's Silver Songsters. He met the neatly-suited boys – many of whom came from South Wales – in 1942 at the Empire Theatre in Bristol, where they were performing in the panto Cinderella. Rex particularly recalled one of the songsters, Ronnie Ronalde, now living in New Zealand, with whom he hoped to organise a reunion.

A letter arrived from a former Songster called Higgins, who lives in Selby, Yorkshire. He was in the troupe from 1944–7 and was keen to contact Rex. And Margaret Knapp e-mailed to say: 'I was five years old, sitting in the front row of the circle watching that very same production of Cinderella at the Empire, convinced that Randolph Sutton was singing just to me! What memories, and I still love the theatre.' Another letter floated in from Joan Craven in Basingstoke, Hampshire, who appeared with the Songsters in the 1940–1 Revue of Nations. ''I'd love to be reunited with Ronnie Ronalde,' she says, 'if he remembers me after all these years.'

Now living in retirement on the Isle of Wight, Rex appeared in variety shows all over the country with such top names as Bud Flanagan, Max Wall and guitarist Bert Weedon. Clearly, he hasn't forgotten much about those innocent days of variety theatre. He claims he and his family have been reading the *Daily Mail* ever since he can remember and that he even once belonged to the paper's Teddy Tail Club, wearing the club badge which allowed him free access to Southend Pier. Before my time, but sounds a good deal to me.

Rex Graham (right) with Bud Flanagan

54

10 July 2004

Young explorers in Sweden

Another tale of intrepid young people, found. In April Simon Robinson was looking for the fellow school-leavers with whom he went on an adventurous trip to Arctic Sweden in 1966, as part of the British Schools Exploring Society – run under the aegis of the Royal Geographical Society. 'The organisation aimed to send school-leavers into wild country to carry out scientific research before going on to university or a career, and also to teach us how to fend for ourselves and work as a team in adverse conditions,' explained Simon. 'It was an experience I have never forgotten.'

There were various teams carrying out research in glaciology, biology and surveying, but Simon was one of the thirteen-strong group of 'commandos', whose job was to keep the expedition supplied with food and other provisions while they were camped out in the surrounding icy mountains. They carried 60lb packs across vast distances of rough ground in harsh weather conditions – a real bonding experience, claimed Simon. The picture he sent us showed them all around the last camp fire they had in Arctic Sweden before their return to England. He was already in touch with four of his commando group and was searching for the missing eight.

The item resulted in an enthusiastic letter from Samantha Eve of BSES Expeditions, formerly the British Schools Exploring Society. By chance, BSES is also in the process of tracing their young explorers of yesteryear in time for its seventy-fifth anniversary in 2007. There is a website (www.bses.org.uk) on which members can get in touch with each other. In addition, one of Simon's missing commandos, Frank Savage, has made contact and is keen to speak to Simon. It seems a big celebration is in the offing.

55

26 June 2004

Good news about Lois Hughes's quest for her old childhood friends from Bolton. To re-cap, on VE-Day in May 1945 Lois and her neighbourhood mates on Pedder Street put on a special show for their celebratory street party. As Lois recalled: 'Our mothers arranged a "back-street concert", hanging sheets on washing lines to create a little theatre and building a platform. We commandeered a lot of chairs and charged a small entrance fee. After performing our party pieces, there were refreshments.

'The grand finale was a tableau of us dressed in national

Lois and her pals from Pedder Street, Bolton, celebrate VE-Day

costumes, and as the eldest child I was Britannia, draped in a
Union Jack. A photographer from the Bolton Evening News
came and took a picture of us. It was in the paper the next day
and we were all thrilled. I realised that the event marked
something momentous, but at that age didn't quite understand
the significance of it.'

Lois wrote touchingly about her recollections of the war – a
time of danger and deprivation, but nevertheless the best years of
her life. 'There was real neighbourliness and true friendship,' she
wrote. 'I would love to get in touch with my friends from that
time.' Well, several of those friends have been in touch and there
is to be a reunion soon of the old Pedder Street gang. Lois is
particularly keen to meet up with John Dutton – her 'first love' –
together with his wife, naturally.

56

10 April 2004

We recently featured an item on retired printer Clyde Cartwright's search for fellow ex-members of the Boys Brigade. From 1945–51 he belonged to the 29th London Company, based in Deptford. Clyde wrote enthusiastically: 'There was no telly in those days and not much for young boys to do, so the Brigade played an important role in our lives and organised many activities for us. It was more militaristic and churchy than the scouts, but it was a healthy organisation which got us involved in sports and athletics. We also had a band, and once a year there would be a big display at the Albert Hall. It instilled important Christian values in us and gave us a good grounding in discipline. There was no hanging about in the Boys Brigade.' The godless couch potatoes of today could do with some of that, eh?

The item elicited some equally enthusiastic responses. First up was John Lawson, who recognised himself on the photo – standing far left in second row – and was keen to make contact with his old mate Clyde. Then Les Nelson came over all nostalgic in Orpington, Kent. He, too, was a BB member in the forties – his company was the 155th London, based at Peckham Rye: 'I remember crossing paths with Clyde's company. We played them at football and competed against them in the annual band competition. I'd be delighted to get in touch with Clyde and share a few memories from Brigade days.'

John Russell, Boys Brigade historian and editor of the BB magazine The Onlooker, got quite excited too, and offered to help Clyde in his quest. And lastly John Bates, secretary of an

*29th London Company of the Boys Brigade with
Clyde Cartwright 4th from left in second row*

organisation for ex-BB members, found it a 'wonderful surprise'
that his favourite newspaper column had at last featured the BB.
'We are always keen to enrol more members,' he said. 'I can be
contacted at johna.bates@ntlworld.com.'

57

21 February 2004

A month ago we ran the story of Bill Carr's search for some of the
old RAF pals with whom he served in Celle, northwestern
Germany, in 1956–7. His best chums from those days were
Londoners Peter 'Spider' Fletcher and Ron Lambert, both now

Spider (left) and Ron, fooling about in Germany in the fifties

in their mid-sixties. He was also hoping to track down two other RAF pals, George 'Geordie' Merifield and Jacko Jackson. Good nicknames.

They lost touch when the RAF station at Celle was handed back to the Germans in 1957 and the servicemen split up and went their separate ways. 'It never occurred to us,' Ron reflected, 'to exchange addresses at the time. But having lived and served together for a year and been a part of each other's lives, it would be great to meet up to talk about the past and to see how life has treated them.'

Well, three out of four isn't a bad result. Firstly, Ron Lambert wrote in from Gillingham, Dorset. He described his 'complete and utter shock' at seeing the ancient photo of himself and 'Spider' fooling about, pretending to perform a rock 'n' roll act, using broomsticks for guitars. The exuberant pair had been billeted together at Celle. He was very pleased at being reunited with Bill, his fellow 'cop'. Then an e-mail blew in from Geordie Merifield, now a retired traffic warden living in Margate, Kent, who is equally keen on arranging a long overdue get-together. This was followed by an e-mail from old Spider himself, who nowadays lives in Reading. So now we await word from Jacko.

58

7 February 2004

A happy ending to the story we published shortly before Christmas, regarding the two boyhood friends from post-war Hartlepool. Andrzej Szmidt and his mother had fled from Poland to Russia as refugees at the start of the Second World War. They later managed to reach Iraq and Uganda, finally arriving in England in May, 1945. Andrzej's father, an officer in the Polish Navy, had escaped to England during the war and served on Polish warships escorting convoys from the USA and Russia. At war's end these ships were based in Hartlepool, which is why Andrzej and his mother came here.

The reunited Szmidts rented a room from the Horsefield family at their home in Belmont Gardens, West Hartlepool, and Andrzej and the Horsefields' son Donald became close friends. The pair went to school together at Elwick Road Boys' School. Then, in the fifties, the Szmidts returned to a Poland in the grip of the Cold War (a bad idea, methinks) and lost contact with the Horsefields.

Andrzej is now the sixty-five-year-old property manager for a shopping centre in the Polish town of Gdynia. Through an

Donald (left) and Andrzej at Hartlepool docks in the forties

English friend, Paul Humberston, he contacted us to see if we could trace his long-lost childhood chum Donald. The item in this column was read by Donald's wife, who gasped in amazement, called out 'That's you!' and passed her hubby the paper. Now a retired headmaster in Manchester, Donald was thrilled to have been 'found'. He rang Andrzej in Gdynia on Christmas Day – the first time they had spoken to each other in fifty years. What a brilliant Christmas present for them both.

59

17 January 2004

More from the RAF. Michael 'Curly' Ballard (you could tell from his photo how he got the nickname) served with the force in the Canal Zone in Egypt from 1951–3, where he worked as an engine mechanic servicing aircraft arriving from Britain. The planes often brought showbiz personalities on their way to entertain the British troops then stationed in Egypt. The Queen Mum arrived once during Curly's tenure and in 1952 his squadron serviced the Canberra aircraft on its record-breaking flight to Australia.

'We were a happy bunch,' he reminisced, 'but because of the local troubles at that time our movements were restricted and we counted the days until our return to the UK.' Curly was eager to trace his ex-comrades from those days. 'There were many characters around, for example Corporal Jones, who used to kill flies and eat them and included flowers in his diet. The others included Ben Lowman, Yorky Taylor, Tony Walkden and Taff Pounder. There were also airmen who had served in the Second

World War, such as Scouse Crewson, who had to borrow kit for inspections, as he had sold all his kit except for what he stood up in. I'd love to know what happened to these people.'

We could tell him for sure what's happened to two of them. First up, Tony Walkden e-mailed from Aberdeen to say he was intrigued to read the item and astounded to see himself 'mentioned in dispatches' along with other long-lost pals. He was glad for the chance to

RAF man Curly Ballard in Egypt in the fifties

re-unite with Curly & co. Tony recalled his days in the Canal Zone with some fondness, although it wasn't an easy time: 'A few of us had motorbikes and made trips to places like the Blue Lagoon and Ismalia, which were most enjoyable. Sadly, though, we also experienced the early stages of terrorism. Several dispatch riders died as a result of steel wires stretched across roads.' Ken Ashy, from Newmarket, Suffolk, was another of Curly's RAF mates. They shared the same billet. He contacted us to say he'd definitely be up for a chinwag about old times.

60

10 January 2004

Roy Grant's quest to track down some of the former child actors who had appeared with him in the 1953 production of The King and I at London's Drury Lane Theatre has met with some success. Now a retired teacher from Brighton, Roy recalled his thespian days in the hit musical and how its juvenile cast worked perhaps even harder than the adults: 'Because not only did we do eight performances a week, leaving the theatre at 11 pm each night, we all had to be at our various schools throughout London by nine o'clock the following morning. Holidays such as Easter and Christmas did not exist and the only time we had to ourselves was on Sundays.

'Nevertheless for two years, although we were all crammed into just two dressing rooms, we never had any differences. Issues such as race, creed or class never affected us, we were just kids of all nationalities who were thrown together and had a lot of fun. We're in our sixties now. What different lives we must have led, and what stories we could tell.'

Barry Barnett e-mailed to say it was a wonderful surprise to see the item – a real blast from his past. He is standing on the far left in the second row. Now a London cabbie of some 30 years' standing (well, sitting, really) he had vivid, happy memories of his King & I days. 'The show was a huge success,' he said proudly. 'One of the highlights for me was meeting its composers, Rodgers and Hammerstein, when they visited London. But the acting business is so precarious. I left it when I started a family and needed more financial security. Seems like another lifetime now.'

The cast of child actors in The King and I, Drury Lane, 1953

Contact was also made by other members of the cast: twin sisters Daphne Lousvet and Joyce Long, Gloria Peverett and Miriam Jacobs. Looks like a showbiz reunion is on the cards. Mwa-mwa, dahlings . . .

61

3 January 2004

Back in September we ran the story of Ken and Joan Leeson's search for the Best Man at their wedding in 1954. Earlier, as teenagers in the forties, they had been great pals and took their

Ken Leeson today, retired and living in Eastbourne

first holiday together sans parents. As Ken recalled: 'We managed to save up enough money and decided to go to Ramsgate. Because we had never stayed in a hotel in our lives, my mother sat us down and explained how and when to use the right knives, forks, etc. so that we wouldn't disgrace ourselves at mealtimes.'

They lost touch sometime in the sixties after several house moves, but with Ken and Joan's golden wedding anniversary coming up this year, naturally they were eager to share the happy occasion with their long-lost friend and Best Man. But it turned out to be one of those rare cases of an old chum being sought who is found, but refuses for some mysterious reason to renew the friendship. I won't even mention his name, in case it offends his reticent nature. Let's call him X.

The item was read by Derek and June Virtue, who could barely believe their eyes. You see, X was Best Man at *their* wedding, too, in 1955. And they, too, had been out of touch with him for many years. Then one day they stumbled across his name in a phone book and rang him up. X told them in no uncertain terms that he did not wish to see them again, despite the fact that he and Derek had been good buddies in their youth. Derek was very disappointed, not to mention utterly mystified. But he respected his old friend's wishes and let the matter drop.

In response to the item, the Virtues got in touch and passed on X's contact details to the Leesons. Perhaps, they reasoned, the secretive and unsociable Best Man had changed his views on old friendships. Dear readers, he hadn't. The messages Ken left for him went unanswered.

Half a century ago all three of them – Ken, Derek and X, had worked together as teenaged motorcycle messengers for the Post Office in Woolwich, south London. Happily, this column has now reunited two of them. Ken and Derek plan to meet up soon and will have much to chat about, not least of all the mysterious Mr X.

62

20 December 2003

What a fine response to Norman 'Jock' Muir's request for us to help trace his erstwhile fellow members of the football team of HMS *Ajax* from the mid-sixties. An ace team on a happy ship, they played some forty matches, losing only five, and were the proud holders of the Small Ships' Cup. Norman served for nine 'eventful' years in the Royal Navy, seeing service in the Med, West Indies, South America, Far East and Mauritius. Now aged sixty and living in Bickleigh, near Plymouth – with 42 Commando of the Royal Marines based across the field at the bottom of his garden – Jock was hoping to organise a reunion for the football-playing lads after all these years.

I can report that it looks like being a jolly affair. Bob Smith was first to spot himself in our photo of the team – he's in the front row, sitting to the captain's left. Now sixty-two, Bob spent many

HMS Ajax *football squad, 1965–6*

years in the London Fire Brigade after leaving the Navy, and he's looking forward to getting together with the rest of the lads.

John Wise also got in touch. An Ajax crew member from 1965 to 1967, he recalled that, as well as the footballers, the ship had a first class water polo team which won many games against Singaporean and Malaysian teams. He had fond memories of his years on the ship and recognised many of the faces in the photo. Then there was Frank Nunn, who remembered Jock from another of his naval postings and hoped to meet up with him.

Plans for the old sea-dogs' reunion are gathering pace.

63

9 August 2003

It didn't take long to reunite several long-lost members of the Merlin Grove mob – a gang of kids who grew up together on a street in Beckenham, South London, in the forties and fifties. Two of them, Dave Baker, a sixty-five-year-old telecommunications worker from Tonbridge, Kent, and Jack Nightingale, now living in Australia, were keen to trace their old street pals.

Merlin Grove mob members Dave Baker (left) and Jack Nightingale

The gang had an adventurous Second World War. Merlin Grove was hit by a parachute mine and several houses were demolished. In their place a POW camp was erected, and although the POWs were not German, but Italian, to the kids they were 'just a bunch of Krauts' and when the prisoners were being marched down the road, the Merlin Grove mob would fall in behind them, goose-stepping and giving the Nazi salute.

We published their story in June, and received several eager responses. One was from mob member Arthur Gould, who remembered Dave and Jack well. 'Thanks for the unexpected trip down memory lane.' he said. Another was from Marcia Burn, sixty-three, also of the gang. 'I look back on those days as happy and carefree,' she told us. 'With no TV, we played rounders in the street, picnicked on Hayes Common and put on plays in my back garden. I had a long chat with Dave and it all came flooding back. Marvellous.'

For good measure, there was also an e-mail from Beckenham resident and author Pat Manning, who is gathering material for a book on the area, likes the mob's story and hopes to include it in her book. So, fame at last for those street kids of yesteryear. And what about an agent's fee for me?

64

7 June 2003

A month ago we ran the story of Jonathan Bagram's search for his two daughters, now eighteen and twenty, who he hadn't seen for seventeen years due to the break-up of his relationship with their mother. Jonathan, a health care consultant living in east

Jonathan Bagram

London, has been happily married for several years to his wife Lorraine, with whom he has two small sons. But he has always been deeply saddened by the absence in his life of the girls, Sherree and Roni. He suspected that perhaps they wanted nothing to do with him.

'I've often thought of them,' wrote Jonathan, 'and how sad it was that they were growing up without their father. I feel guilty about the way things have turned out, and that I haven't been in touch with them, but it's not through lack of trying.'

I'm very pleased to report that following the publication of the item on his story, his daughter Sherree contacted him and they spoke on the phone for a long time. 'It was great,' said Jonathan. 'It was the first time we had spoken in seventeen years and I was so happy about it. We arranged to meet the following week, together with my other daughter, Roni.'

He admitted that the meeting was a little strange at first, understandably enough in view of the circumstances. 'We were only going to spend an hour together, but before we knew it three hours had gone by. They now have my address and phone numbers, so I am hoping they'll get in touch again soon. They know how much I'd like to see them, but I am going to leave it up to them. I'd love for my sons Oscar and Ryan to meet their sisters one day soon.'

65

17 May 2003

Back in the fifties and early sixties Trevor Collins had a semi-professional dance band which played regular gigs at the various US army camps in the London area. Calling himself Dene Trevor, he led the band and performed the vocals, singing the

Dance band, with Trevor at the microphone,
Ron Gibson sitting at back in white hat

hits of the era – songs made famous by the likes of Frankie Laine and Frankie Vaughan, Billy Daniels and Johnny Ray.

They once appeared on Hughie Greene's TV show *Opportunity Knocks*. 'We came second,' said Trevor, now aged seventy, 'having lost out to a man who played the spoons, which was a bit embarrassing, really.'

The band members lived in the Surrey area, and when, in around 1965 they all started moving away to different parts of the country due to their day-jobs, they reluctantly disbanded. Trevor himself moved to Dorset, where he bought a furniture business.

Now, after thirty-eight years, he has been reunited with his erstwhile drummer Ron Gibson, who has settled in Bognor Regis after many years playing the cruise liners. At seventy-four he is still drumming in various local musical groups. 'It was great to see him again. We didn't stop talking at our reunion, about our gigs and the fun we used to have.'

66

10 May 2003

In March we published former BOAC steward Ken Brown's search for the British girl who had once asked him to give a fan letter to Beatle George Harrison. The year was 1964 and the place was the tarmac at Bangkok Airport, where the Fab Four's plane had stopped

Nan as a teenager

Nan's fan letter to George Harrison

briefly *en route* to Sydney, Australia, amid a mad scramble of fans and news reporters.

As Ken recalled: 'They allowed the embassy kids to come on to the tarmac to see the pop group. But the rush from the teenagers was so great that they had to pull the aircraft steps away, so the kids couldn't see their idols, who were stuck inside the first class cabin. I was on the tarmac at the time and an attractive girl from the British Embassy who looked about sixteen gave me a letter and begged me to make sure George Harrison got it. When I got back on the plane I did give it to George, who read it and gave it back to me, with the words "Save it for your grandchildren".

'It has sat in a drawer for nearly forty years, and now that I've retired from British Airways after twenty-five years' service, my thoughts have turned back to those early days. With George now dead, I'd like to return the letter to its author. Her name was Nan Desmond and she lived at the British Embassy in Bangkok. In her letter she wrote that she was born in Scotland and that she had met George at a party in Liverpool in 1961. I hope you can help me find Nan, so that I can send her the letter. I'm sure it would bring back fond memories.'

Mission accomplished. Nan (now a fifty-two-year-old grand-mother living in Kent and working for British Telecom) saw the item in this column and was flabbergasted. 'I remember writing that letter, but after all these years, can't recall the contents. That event on the tarmac caused quite a stir. The next day my picture appeared on the front page of the *Bangkok Times* and my dad went berserk, threatening to smash all my pop records.' Fond memories, indeed.

67

8 March 2003

Last month Len Dimelow was searching for his buddies from 245 Signals Squadron at Cyrenaica in Benghazi, North Africa, in 1959–61. The lads were doing their National Service and having a great time, appearing in comedy sketches in the variety shows staged by their squadron.

We reproduced a photo of their Desert Goons sketch, and one of the Goons, Dave Hobbs, nearly choked on his cornflakes when he recognised himself in the picture. He was very happy to have word again of his old pals after so many decades, and is looking forward to meeting up with them this spring.

Like Len, Dave left the army in 1961 and joined British Telecom as an engineer. He took early retirement in 1995 and now lives in Ipswich. 'Seeing your article brought back a lot of wonderful memories,' Dave told us, 'and Len and I had a long

Desert Goons comedy sketch, with Dave Hobbs on far right

chat on the phone. Funnily enough, we each remembered different things about those days. I guess memory is very subjective. That era in my life was a sort of yardstick for everything that came after. I think it's a shame that they stopped National Service, because it was a very good thing for young men – not so much for the discipline, as for the real comradeship you share. It just doesn't happen on civvie street.'

68

25 January 2003

Last month we ran the story of the 'mystery family' who had a holiday in Mousehole, Cornwall, in the summer of 1979, and left a lasting impression on a couple they met there, Tom Neale and his wife. They were all staying at the renowned Lobster Pot Hotel, and the two little girls who belonged to this family took a real shine to Tom.

Just before departing, Tom took a picture of the family, and to his surprise the girls presented him with small gifts made of china. He never forgot them, and has kept the gifts all these

The Flowers with daughters (from left to right) Ali, Alex and Sarah

years. He had been wondering whatever became of the children and wanted to trace them so that he could repay the touching gesture with gifts of his own. But he never knew their names.

Well, the family didn't remain a mystery for long. An e-mail flew in from Sarah Cavell, the teenager in the mystery family. She explained that that holiday in Cornwall was an important part of her early memories. Her mother Liz had married her stepfather Richard Flower the previous year and it was their first holiday as a family.

'My sister Ali was eight and stepsister Alex nine. We all remember "Uncle Tom" and still talk about him when we recall that distant holiday. All three of us have children of our own now. We're so touched that Tom still remembers us, as well, and would love to be in contact with him. Sadly, my mother and stepfather both died in the nineties. Having lost our parents, memories from past happy times are even more important.'

69

18 January 2003

Good news about Brian Hilton's search for old friends from the fifties with whom he formed the London skiffle group, the Metropolitans. The group used to play gigs at such popular venues as the Skiffle Cellar and the Two I's Coffee Bar in Old Compton Street, Soho, and had many impromptu jam sessions with the likes of Adam Faith, Wee Willie Harris and Johnny Kidd. Heady days.

'We called ourselves the Metropolitans after our usual method

The Metropolitans, from left to right:
Harry, Pete, Len, Mac and Dave

of transport, the Metropolitan tube line, on which we often entertained the passengers and passed the hat around afterwards. After late-night gigs we would try to get taxis, but on seeing my double bass the cabbies usually looked the other way. So I'd hide in shop doorways until the taxi had stopped, then appear when it was too late for the driver to ignore us.'

The group broke up in 1959, and the members mostly went their separate ways and lost touch. But forty years on two of the long lost Metropolitans, Harry Maynard and Len Thompson, have turned up alive and kicking, after seeing Brian's item in this column.

Brian wrote: 'I had a lovely chat with Harry, who lives with his wife at Morden, Surrey, in the same house they bought when they married in the early sixties. He's sixty-six now and still working as a draughtsman. They've stayed good friends with Len and his wife Tina, who live only a couple of miles away at Worcester Park. Len seems to be a gentleman of leisure these days. Amazingly, the four of them had a holiday in Symonds Yat, Herefordshire, when my wife and I were living there in the eighties, and stayed a mere half-mile away from our cottage. We often walked our dogs past the place they were staying in and could easily have bumped into them . . . but didn't.'

Together with fellow Metropolitan member Dave Bergin – whom Brian had tracked down earlier – the newly reunited skiffle pals plan to meet in the New Year. 'Our collective memories should be able to fill the gaps in our recollections of our youth and a wonderful, long-gone era,' said a wistful Brian.

70

21 December 2002

Two months ago we published the story about Mancunian Gerard Sykes, who was hoping to trace the sons of his cousin Alfred Murdoch, killed while serving with the Wiltshire Regiment during the Second World War. Alfred grew up in Poplar, east London, was a Millwall football club supporter and worked as a 'nippy' at a Lyon's Corner House before the war. Often during the summer holidays he would go north to stay with Gerard and his family, who lived in Salford. Gerard recalled: 'He was a few years older than me. I think the last time I saw him was the summer of 1935, when he was about eighteen. I remember we watched a rugby game, but he didn't much care

Alfred Murdoch with wife and sons Peter (on left) and John in 1940

for it; he only liked football. Soon afterwards he married and moved to Basingstoke. When war broke out he joined up. By then he had his sons, John and Peter. I believe he was killed in 1941. His sons would be in their sixties now.' An ancestor of Alfred's had a pub, the Crown Inn in Salford, in Victorian times, and Gerard has some mementoes from it, as well as family photographs, documents, books and a painting. He's been a willing guardian of the Murdoch family history, but now hopes to pass these items on to their rightful heirs.

As it happened, rightful heir John Murdoch was visiting his grandsons in Dubai when the piece came out in this column, and he received a phone call from home to tell him about it. On his return he found that the whole family was bubbling with excitement. John and Peter had had no idea that they even had relations in the North of England. They were very young when their father died, and their mother remarried and hardly told them anything about their paternal background.

Gerard updated us: 'When they came to visit us recently, John and Peter were literally amazed at what they learnt about their father's family. We had a very enjoyable – and emotional – time, with plenty of champagne and an excellent meal. It was brilliant.'

71

7 December 2002

I'm happy to report that Brian Deakin and Gerry Freedman – chums from the sixties, when both were working for Willerby's the Tailors in Hull – have been reunited after a thirty-year separation. Brian, who used to work in the insurance business, is retired and lives in Stockton-on-Tees. Sadly, he is now widowed. We featured the story of his search for Gerry a couple of months ago, and on the day the piece appeared, I received an e-mail from Gerry, asking excitedly to be put in touch with his old friend and colleague. The e-mail was sent from his home in Beaumont, Texas (an hour from Houston) where he has been living since 1986. He works as a consultant engineer for a major oil company engaged in offshore exploration and production of deep-water oilfields. Sounds serious.

He had heard about the item in this column from *Daily Mail* reader Claire Noyce, who explained that Gerry and Heather Freedman are her brother's parents-in-law. She wasted no time in e-mailing the Freedman family to let them know about it.

So, the messages whizzed backwards and forwards across cyber-space and soon Brian and Gerry were reminiscing about their old times as men-about-town together in the northeast: going to the greyhound races at Brough Park in Newcastle, followed by

Brian and Valerie Deakin on their wedding day in 1959

dancing at the Oxford Galleries, where for some reason the pair were nicknamed the Likely Lads. And why would that have been? I think we should be told . . .

72

9 November 2002

Frances (wearing glasses) and Pamela in Norwood days

Frances Gibbs and Pamela Leff, who spent many years as childhood friends at the Norwood Jewish Children's Home in West Norwood, London, have been reunited again after four decades.

They have fond memories of their days at Norwood (which was built by the Rothschild family, originally as a hospital). 'We didn't have families of our own,' remarked Frances, who was taken into care at the age of seven, 'but at the Home we were like one big family. Pam and I belonged to the netball team and played against the north London Jewish clubs. Each year we'd go on a taxi outing to Brighton with a lot of London cabbies and their families. It was always a great occasion which we would talk about for weeks afterwards.' Could those outings have influenced Frances in her later choice of occupation as a cab driver? Hmm.

'At fifteen I was sent to live with my mother in the East End of London, but sadly, it didn't work out and I ended up getting married very young. It was the sixties, and we set up home in

Hackney. I've been lucky – my husband and I have been together for forty-one years and have three children. Not bad for a teenage bride!' Frances now lives in Pevensey Bay, East Sussex, where she has been driving her own cab. She recently gave it up in favour of being a volunteer driver for the NHS Trust.

Only a few days after the appearance of her story in this column, she received a surprise phone call from her old Norwood friend, now Mrs Pamela Shaw. It turned out that someone from the Norwood Old Scholars' Association, who knows Pamela, read the piece and got in touch with her. As Frances subscribes to the association's newsletter, it wasn't difficult to obtain her phone number. 'We didn't stop talking for an hour on the phone – goodness knows what we'll be like at our forthcoming Norwood reunion in Essex. It has been such a thrill getting back together with Pam.'

73

26 October 2002

Our recent story about Brian Fuller, who had for years been trying to find former classmates from Galliard Road Primary School in Edmonton, north London – which he attended during the Second World War – reaped a nice crop of enthusiastic letters and e-mails from his old school pals.

Of course, it's not surprising so many of them remember their early schooldays, lived out as they were against a dramatic back-drop of bombing raids, sirens, air battles and gunfire, with many long sessions spent in the school's murky air raid shelter.

'In 1940 I was six years old,' he said, 'and despite that tender

Brian Fuller's class in 1945; he is fourth from the left in the back row

age I can still clearly remember the Battle of Britain and the Blitz. In those days most of us could read and write at a very early age, and I would write and tell little stories in one of the school's air raid shelters while the sirens, aircraft and gunfire outside made it both frightening and exciting. I also held hands with a certain Shirley Diss, whilst our teacher read a book called Mystery at Witchend which I had brought in to school.'

John Hall was among those who wrote to us in response to the item. He explained that the school had been in a particularly vulnerable area during the war: 'As well as a small-arms factory, there was also an electrical plant, railway yard and reservoir nearby. It made life for us rather exciting.' By coincidence, both he and Brian went into the newspaper printing trade when they grew up. Now retired, John lives in Lymington, Hampshire, while Brian is in Holland-on-Sea, Essex.

The item in the column also helped locate one of Brian's best-remembered classmates, Pauline Berridge, now Pauline Cox. The sixty-eight-year-old retired schoolteacher lives near Totnes in Devon. 'I recall Brian very well,' she says. 'As well as telling some rather good stories, he was also a train enthusiast and could draw trains very well. It will be great getting together again, but my goodness it all seems so very long ago . . . '

74

12 October 2002

Great news of a successful outcome for one of our more poignant family stories. Back in June I wrote about Linda Anne Walker, forty-eight-year-old nurse in Adelaide, Australia, who, together with her five siblings, was desperate to find the mother who had walked out on the family forty years earlier. They had just emigrated from England to Australia in 1962, when Beatrice Shirley disappeared from the lives of husband Bill and their six children, aged between three and ten. Nobody knew why. Bill couldn't bring them up alone, so the youngsters were put into various care homes. Family life was over. In Linda's moving letter, she wrote of how deeply she had always sensed her mother's absence: 'Every milestone in my life has been punctuated by the questions: where's Mum? is she thinking about me? what would she say about this? wouldn't she be proud? I've been searching for her all my adult life. It would be wonderful to see her again. She's a grandmother many times over and even a great-granny now. I do hope it isn't too late to find her.'

Beatrice and Bill Shirley with their children on board the ship
bound for Australia in 1962

Linda had been informed that many years earlier Beatrice had
returned to England, changed her name and was living alone
somewhere in London. Linda sent a UK contact a list of possible
individuals to visit and check out, armed with the item about
Beatrice in this column. The very first woman visited was duly
staggered on seeing the picture and cried out: 'That's me!' She
phoned Linda in Australia the same day and they had a moving

conversation – the first in four decades. It was the outcome Linda had prayed for.

As to why her mother disappeared in the first place, that will doubtless take a little time to emerge. Meanwhile, Linda and her brothers and sisters are still 'on a high'.

75

5 October 2002

Back in July we ran a piece about the vice-chairman of the Leyton Orient Supporters' Club, Steve Jenkins, and his search for relatives of footballer George Scott, who played for the team from 1908 to 1915, the year when all league football ceased temporarily due to the First World War. Steve has been researching into this period of the team's history – at that time it was still called Clapton Orient, and it was the first English league club to join up *en masse*. Forty members and staff volunteered to fight, and sadly, three of the team's finest footballers were killed in the Battle of the Somme in 1916. One of them was Scott.

On Saturday 30 April, 1921, the Prince of Wales (later King Edward VIII) visited Millfields Road to see Orient play Notts County, a match which Orient won 3–0. History was made that day, as it was the first time a member of royalty had ever attended a Football League match. The royal visit was to show gratitude for Clapton Orient's patriotic example during the Great War.

Disappointingly, none of Scott's relatives has yet been traced, but there have been helpful responses to the column from descendants of others footballers who played for Clapton Orient in the early part of the twentieth century, which Steve, as the team's historian, found quite fascinating.

Some members of the Leyton Orient football team pre-1915

One letter arrived from Mrs Paula Sherlock, whose father, E. W. Sibley, played for the team at around the turn of the century. 'I can remember his talking enthusiastically about Clapton Orient,' she writes. 'I believe he went with the club to introduce football to the Belgians, where, as I recall, they had to play on cinders. He told me the changing room looked like a slaughter-house when the game was over . . .'

CHAPTER SIX

Still Missing . . .

The following stories, which appeared in the column over the past three years, are about people who are still 'long lost'. If any readers know the missing people involved and can help us reunite them with those who are looking for them, I would be most obliged.

And here's a little teaser. Fourteen of the fifteen stories are genuine, but one is fictitious. The one I've invented contains a factual error which the eagle-eyed will be able to spot. If you think you know which story is made up and can correct the error in it, send a postcard to me at the Letters Department, Daily Mail, Northcliffe House, 2 Derry Street, London W8 5TT, UK. Include your address. The writers of the first three postcards I receive (which must arrive by 31 December, 2010) will be sent a £35 book voucher. The winners will be announced in the column soon afterwards.

Who says this book isn't fun?

1

Carole (left) and Mary on holiday in Devon the fifties

Carole Large, née Burgess, would like to trace the friend she met as a child whilst on holiday in Brixham, Devon, in the fifties. 'Her name at the time was Mary Cook,' writes Carole, 'and she came from Bexleyheath in Kent. We were about eight or nine when we first met and our families used to stay at the same place, the Bay View Holiday Camp. We met up there each year and kept in contact in between times by letter. Then we lost touch and I've often wondered what happened to her. It isn't much to go on, I'm afraid. I am sixty-three now, so it was a long time ago. I lived in Stopsley in Luton then, as I do now.

'Mary was slightly older than me and I tended to look up to her. I think her parents were real Londoners, which I found quite fascinating, although my Luton accent often leads people to think I come from London. At the holiday camp we stayed in caravans and joined in the weekly evening events in the small clubhouse. These would have been Beetle Drives, Talent Shows and Cafe Continental. Mary and I were allowed to go shopping together and we bought girly things like nail polish or lipstick that we thought dreadfully grown up. I remember going mackerel fishing together and Mary's mum cooked us the mackerel the following day – it was the first time I ever tasted it.

'We must have lost touch sometime before 1960. Unfortunately I didn't keep any of Mary's letters and I cannot remember her address. I still go to Brixham regularly and have done so all my life. I wonder if Mary still visits it, too?'

2

An e-mail arrives from seventy-year-old Margaret Lovell of Bristol: 'I get great pleasure reading the Missing and Found column on Saturdays (the only day I'm able to take the *Daily Mail*) and would be so grateful if you could find a dear friend from the early sixties. Her name is Joyce Brown and she came from Bridlington in Yorkshire.

'We met at the Slade School of Fine Art, part of University College London, in 1961. Her specialisation was painting, whereas I did sculpture. My photo shows us in the studio with a life-size study I was working on in clay. Joyce is on

Margaret (right) and Joyce at the Slade School of Art, 1961

the left. We had some great adventures together and once hitch-hiked to Greece in the summer holidays. This was before mass tourism and we travelled on "half a shoestring" in order to see the ancient sites in Athens and Crete. 'I graduated in 1962, a year before Joyce, and went to Italy for a year on a scholarship. I only saw Joyce a couple of times after that, as she stayed on in London – by that time she had her baby daughter Vanessa, who would be about forty-five years old now. My own life, meanwhile, has revolved around sculpture and I've recently had a book published about my work. I'd love to see Joyce again – she is even mentioned in the book!'

3

'I was adopted as a baby,' writes James Williamson, who is retired and lives in Malaga, Spain, 'and have been looking for my birth mother and siblings for about forty-five years now. Sadly, it has proved impossible. I've always hoped that one day some member of my family might try to trace me. However, it's possible they do not even know I exist. I think the only way I am going to crack this is with the help of a national newspaper.

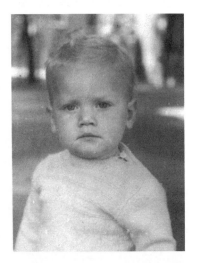

James Williamson as a small boy in the late forties

'I was born Michael John Taylor, on 25 March, 1948, in Lewisham Hospital, south London, and adopted by Ivy and Jim Williamson, who re-named me James Alfred Williamson. I'm looking for my mother Ellen Taylor, née Smith, and her four children: Pauline, Irene, Ronald and Sheila. At the time of my birth Ellen was twenty-nine. She knew the Williamson family, and Ivy and Jim adopted me directly through her, not through an agency.

'After my adoption, Ellen vanished with her remaining children. It's possible that the other children were illegitimate, as was I, with different fathers and therefore different surnames. If anyone can help, please do so soon, before it's too late. It might already be too late to find Ellen, but to find my brother and sisters would be wonderful.'

James has passionate views on adoption and other childhood issues and has written a book dealing with them, called They Can't Touch Him Now. His website is www.jameswilliamson-taylor.com.

4

Valerie and Mike enjoying the good life in France, 1980

Back in the seventies and eighties Mike Geddes enjoyed summer holidays in the South of France, where his cousin Valerie Simms lived an idyllic life in a seventeenth century farmhouse complete with small vineyard. 'She'd inherited money from her father in about 1975,' says Mike, 'and being a bit of a hippy, decided to up sticks from "boring England" and settle in the Bordeaux region. She was ahead of her time, beating all the ex-pats who re-located to France in later decades. And she loved it there. She had friends all over the place and someone was always visiting.

'I was younger than Val and she seemed so glamorous to me. The sort of person who floats through life quite easily, having a nice time. The usual rules didn't apply. She had once done some modelling, but other than that she never seemed to have to work at anything. It was different for me – I worked hard in London to earn my living in advertising. There was always a lot of pressure.'

After Mike married and started a family, there were fewer visits to Valerie's idyll. He was busy forging his own life here and as the years passed the contact between him and his cousin became sporadic. 'I last spoke to her in 1994. I'd just seen the Queen and President Chirac on TV, opening the Channel Tunnel. So I rang her and said I planned to take the family to France on Eurostar the following year and travel down to see her. She said "what a good idea". But it never happened because a year later she sold up and moved, without telling me where she went. It might have had something to do with the Frenchman she was involved with at the time. So is Val still in France, back in the UK or somewhere else? I'd love to know and to see her again.'

5

Ray (on right) with actor Georgie Saunders

'Where to start!' exclaims Ray Lovegrove. 'In the sixties I worked in the music business, starting in 1964 as a roadie for the Kinks. Afterwards I worked for the record producer Shel Talmy, and in 1967 I was resident DJ at the Cromwellian Club, where I befriended many musicians and actors. The following year I managed the Marquee Club for a while. On my photo I am on the right, with the actor Georgie Saunders, who appeared in The Saint TV series, I think as Roger Moore's manservant. I've often wondered how he's got on through the years. It would be great to meet up for a chat.

'The Rolls Royce in the photo was owned by Shel Talmy, who produced the Kinks, the Who and Manfred Mann. I was his PA and driver (I'm still in touch with him – he lives in Los Angeles). I was chummy with Jimi Hendrix, as well as the musician Jeff Beck, with whom I stayed for a while in his flat in Wallington. We would cruise around in the Rolls and – not many people know this – the Imperial War Museum was Jeff's favourite haunt! I wonder how he is these days.

'I crashed that lovely Rolls at three o'clock one morning in South Kensington as I was taking Keith Moon back to his home in Regent's Park. The accident happened when Keith, who was sitting in the back seat, suddenly clamped his hands over my eyes and said "Guess who!" ' Yup, that sounds like crazy Keith all right. 'There are many actors and musicians I'd love to see and chat to again, although a lot have succumbed to drugs and early deaths. Well, I'm sixty-five now, so I guess it's my time to get something back from the State!'

In the seventies Ray moved to Wales, went into the car trade and married the comely Georgina Kerler, who was Miss Wales 1975. They've been together for thirty-three years and now run a residential care home in Devon. Can you imagine a more dramatic career switch for an erstwhile sixties rock dude?

6

Alan, wife and baby in 1971

Alan Dumbell seeks our help in locating his great friend Brian Sumbler, who was his assistant manager when they both worked at Tandy's Hi Fi store in the Old Swan area of Liverpool back in the seventies. 'We often went drinking together in the pubs of Liverpool,' says Alan, 'and spent many evenings contemplating what we would do when we were rich. I was already married to my wife Pauline at the time, and we all got on so well together.

'Brian and I were last in touch when he lived in Cambridge in the late seventies. I do believe he married a girl from Chicago called Janet, then soon afterwards left for America, but I have no idea where. After I left Tandy's I continued in the retail trade for a while, then worked as a sales rep for Green Shield Stamps, travelling the length and breath of Britain with a successful sales team. It was at about this time that Brian and I lost touch.

'We had some great times together, lots of fun, and I still think of him often. I'd love to see him again. I now live in Milton Keynes, have been happily married for the past forty-two years, and have three grandchildren. I'd be so grateful if you could trace him. It would be great to see how his life has panned out.'

7

Bob Fisher of south London was a serving member of the British Forces in Italy following the cessation of hostilities in 1945. As he explains: 'One day I saw an article in the Eighth Army News about the formation of a travelling show aimed at helping to ease the post-war boredom and anti-climax which many servicemen were feeling at the time. I decided to join it.

Bob Fisher in Over the Page, *Italy, 1945*

'Rehearsals began in Naples and on 10 December 1945 the show, called *Over the Page*, was so much enjoyed that after the curtain fell, flowers were thrown on to the stage from a very appreciative audience. And no wonder: among others, the cast included the late and great Harry Secombe and Spike Milligan.

'If possible, I would very much enjoy hearing from any members of the cast or their relations, or anyone else who watched and still remembers our show. I think I might have enough time for some kind of reunion, although I am now in my ninety-third year. Please accept my thanks for any part you may play in the matter.'

Bob looks spiffy indeed on his old photo, in top hat and tails, performing in the memorable show which so royally entertained the brave men who had just won us the war.

8

Babies of RAF Bruggen, Germany, 1993

Alison Whitaker, thirty-nine, of Tamworth in Staffordshire writes: 'My story isn't as old as most of those in your column but I wonder if you could help trace some people I knew sixteen years ago when I lived in Germany. My then husband Gerry Cepelak was a Tornado navigator stationed with 14 Squadron at RAF Bruggen.

'In that year, 1993, seven children were born in the same

squadron! Five of them, all boys, were born that December at RAF Wegberg Hospital – some of the last babies to be born there before it closed down. I have a wonderful photo of the proud Squadron Commander posing with the children along the nose of a Tornado – it adorned a wall at the Medical Centre at RAF Bruggen – and for a while the Squadron was nicknamed 14 Fertile Squadron. Being away from home we wives grew close and got together regularly, both with our husbands and without them when they were away. We helped each other out when we had no other family to rely on.

'RAF Bruggen itself has since closed down and over the years, with so much moving around, we've all lost touch. With those seven babies turning sixteen this year it would be lovely to meet up again with them and their mums and compare notes. My son's name is Peter Cepelak, and funnily enough most of the boys' names are out of Beatrix Potter – Samuel and Thomas are a couple that I remember. All very odd . . . '

9

Graham Penness in 1957

'For some time now I have been trying to trace Richard Henry Bailey, the only son of Sir Donald Bailey OBE, inventor of the wartime Bailey Bridge,' writes Graham Penness. 'Richard and I served our RAF National Service together in the Air Ministry from 1955 to 1957. He then went to Trinity College, Cambridge, and we lost touch.'

Graham explains what the Bailey Bridge was for those (like me) who didn't know: 'It was designed in 1940 to enable heavy armour to cross rivers, etc., when bridges had been blown up. As a result of his contribution to the war effort he was knighted in 1946 and became Dean of the Royal Military College of Science in 1962. His son Richard and I were called up for National Service in 1955 and posted to the Air Ministry at Horseferry Road in London. There we analysed time-and-motion study data sent from the RAF stations at Wittering and Halton, the idea being to reduce the number of vehicles in use or at least make their use more efficient!

'After demob, while Richard took up his place at Cambridge, I returned to my job as a cost clerk in a footwear-making company in my home town of Rushden, Northants. After an exchange of

Christmas cards we lost touch. I went on to have a career in personnel management. I'm seventy-two now and live a few miles from Chester.'

10

Brian Bradley on right-hand side in the back, Palestine 1946

In 1946 Brian Bradley was a nineteen-year-old serving in Palestine with the 2nd Battalion North Staffordshire Regiment, under canvas at Pardess Hanna, about thirty miles from Haifa. He's hoping we can trace some of his old mates from C Company or the TM Section – especially Dougie Chidlow and a fellow whose surname was Clewes. Brian himself went by the nickname 'Slingum' – how cool is that?

He did a lot of patrolling of beaches to round up the illegal Jewish immigrants pouring into Palestine in the wake of the

Second World War. 'We had to put the Jews into barbed-wire enclosures so they could be de-loused with DDT before being questioned and taken to transit camps,' he explains. 'One of the ships that beached was the Susannah, and conditions on board were horrendous. Some jumped overboard from these refugee ships and drowned. It was a terrible time.'

Slingum has sent us a photo showing him and his comrades taking a cooling watermelon break outside their tent. He served in Palestine for twenty months or so before being posted to Egypt, from where he was demobbed in 1948, after which he was able to return to his electrician's job in Chester.

11

Terry Verdon is trying to trace a teacher friend with whom he lost contact back in 1980. His name is Mark Daniels and he taught at Priory Park Girls' School, Lansdown Road, London SW8. 'We worked together at the school from 1976 to 1980, the year I left,' writes Terry. 'Mark was the school's Head of Social Studies and I was Media Resources Officer. We worked together to make lessons more exciting by producing audio-visual teaching materials.

'This was a time of big changes in politics, music and society as a whole, and as twenty-somethings we used to "put the world to rights" in lively discussions and attend rallies and concerts with other colleagues. My picture was taken at an anti-racism rally we attended in 1978. Mark is on the right, holding the banner, and I am half-kneeling on the ground in the centre. I lost contact with Mark when I went to work in East London in 1980. I am now fifty-three, a self-employed web designer and IT consultant,

Terry and Mark at a rally in 1978

have been married for sixteen years and live in Bedford.

'I would really like to get in contact with Mark again, as I have heard that he may be teaching and/or living in East London. I recently found the home-made leaving card he gave me when I left Priory Park School, which read: "One day your star will shine". We have so much to catch up on, and of course, to reminisce about.'

12

left to right – Diane, Lynne and Bernard,
in Blackpool, summer 1964

Bernard Hope of Sunderland wonders if we can help him find two 'nice girls from Leeds' who he met in the summer of 1964 while on holiday in Lytham-St-Anne's. 'I was with my parents, but I spent most of the holiday with the girls, who were school friends called Diane and Lynne.

'We got on really well together, and my parents only saw me at mealtimes. Lytham was a quiet place, with not much to do, but we tried the crazy golf and other seaside attractions. Blackpool was nearby, so we also went there, spending time on the usual Blackpool amusements. That's where the photo was taken.

'The girls and I kept in touch for a number of years until we all married (I married in 1975), but soon after that contact was lost. I had become a teacher and met my wife through teaching. Diane sent me an engagement present at the time. I've just retired from teaching after thirty-six years at the "chalk face".

'I'm interested in finding the girls again to talk about old times and how our lives have progressed, now that we are entering our sixties. My problem is that, to my embarrassment, I can't remember their surnames. I read your column every Saturday and see how "lost" people are brought back together. I feel that only by your publishing my photo can these two ladies be traced.'

13

Olive Weirs and her daughters, Hong Kong, 1960

Rosamund Carpenter of West Sussex is keen to be reunited with her long-lost friend Olive Weirs, who she knew in Hong Kong from 1957 to 1961. Rosamund's husband worked there for twenty years as a Royal Hong Kong police officer. 'Olive had been a dancer in the early fifties,' writes Rosamund, 'a Windmill girl who then went by the name of Olive Leon. When I knew her she had a Thai partner named Anthony Natannapon. They had two beautiful little girls named Tania and Katia and resided in Stanley, on Hong Kong (Victoria) Island.

'Olive and Anthony split up and Olive went back into show business, placing her little girls with foster parents in Hong Kong while she danced under the name of Rena Starr, travelling to various places in the Far East but mainly to Japan. In 1961, I came home to England with my family on a long leave. On our return six months later, I expected to see Olive, as usual, but she never turned up again and I left Hong Kong permanently fourteen years later without ever having discovered what happened to her or her girls.

'Time has gone by and I've often thought of them. Last week, I found a photo of her and the girls taken at my eldest son's third birthday party in 1960. I know Olive's mother lived in London, but I doubt she is still alive. And as far as I'm aware she had no siblings. I'm surprised Olive never made any attempt to contact me and feel that somehow all was not well. Perhaps someone would be able to shed some light on this, for which I would be grateful . . . '

14

Heather and her friends in the sixties

Heather Shorrock of Kirkham, Lancashire, hopes to trace a work colleague from the sixties. She writes: 'We were five friends: Heather Chesney (me), Kath Craig, Sue Midgeley, Margaret Hedley and Pat Sargentson, who worked together at the Guardian Royal Exchange Assurance Company in Lytham St. Anne's, Lancashire. Kath and Margaret were bridesmaids at my 1971 wedding. Kath and I had our children at the same time and have remained friends, and I recently reconnected with Sue and Pat through the internet and now we too see each other regularly. But Margaret moved away from the area in the seventies, I lost touch with her and have no idea where she is.

'We all used to go out together in the sixties. We particularly enjoyed our visits to a Newcastle nightclub called the Dolce Vita and had a great time being the bright young things. And once we drove up to Newcastle in Pat's battered old van to visit Margaret's parents in Wallsend. We could actually see the road through a hole in the floor of the van – it wouldn't be allowed these days! My photo was taken outside Margaret's house in Wallsend. I'm the skinny one in the (very short) yellow dress.

'I left the Guardian to have my first daughter, Louise, before falling ill to gestational diabetes. It was a traumatic time. But following successful treatment, I went on to have another daughter, Jo. My husband Bob was in a pop group called Beau Geste when we married and I'm still married to him. He's a builder and we have a barn in France which we're renovating. Sue works as a doctor's receptionist, Kath is a teaching assistant and lucky Pat lives in Spain. We'd love to find the missing Margaret, meet up again and learn how her life has panned out now that we are all of *mature* years.'

15

Preston, 1975. From left to right: David Wooding, Tony Kelly, Andy Hoban

Journalist Andy Hoban is eager to find the fellow students with whom he took an NCTJ course (National Council for the Training of Journalists) back in 1974–5. They studied at Preston Polytechnic, now the grander-sounding University of Central Lancashire. 'We were good pals,' Andy recalls, 'and afterwards we all scattered to various local newspapers. I went to the *Birkenhead News*. A few of us kept in touch for a while: Mark Thomas (*Bebington News*), David Wooding and Andy Nott (both with the South Lancashire group of papers) and Tony Kelly, who was based in Kirkby and is now a columnist with the *York Press*.

'I later worked on the *Birmingham Evening Mail, Daily Express* and *Daily Mail,* and am currently night editor of the *Sunday Express.* David is now Associate Editor (Politics) at the *News of the World,* Mark is Editor of the *Liverpool Daily Post* and Andy Nott was chief crime reporter for the *Manchester Evening News* and now writes books. I've also been able to trace Sue Crawford (News Editor at the *News & Star* in Carlisle), David Gudgeon, who until recently worked with her, Peter Doyle (works for Devon County Council) and Jeff Hanson, who is in PR. Other names I recall are Carol Baker, Brenda Mason, Amanda Thomas, Jill Littlewood, Shelley Outhwaite and Judith Griffiths. There were two other girls, one of whom was called Anne.

'We're now in our fifties and it would be great to get everyone together for a long overdue reunion in Preston. The TV series *Life On Mars* reminded me so much of newspaper offices back in the seventies, especially the scruffiness and fag smoke. The daft thing is I miss it sometimes.'

CHAPTER SEVEN

A DIY Guide to Tracing People

The Basics

Whoever you are searching for, it is very important for a successful result to get the basic facts right.

If searching for a friend, first names such as Kitty, Dolly or Gerry are not enough. The electoral rolls use only proper full names. So it is very important to start by establishing the full name of the person you are seeking and not the shortened form or nickname by which you knew them. You might be able to get this information from someone else who knew them, such as a member of their family. If not, look up the births records and find their birth entry, which will give their full name, with a middle initial if they have one. (Of course, you will need to know their approximate age in order to search for their birth record.) Birth records are held online on sites such as ancestry.co.uk, findmypast.co.uk or the National Archives website, or you can search at the nearest library which holds them on microfiche. The records for marriages and deaths are held in the same places.

If searching for a family member, ask other relatives for as much information as possible about them- any names, dates and addresses which might help in your search. If you can, look in family bibles (which sometimes contain helpful inscriptions about relatives and family trees), photo albums and diaries, in case they hold more useful information.

Once you have the necessary starting point – full name and date of birth – you can commence your search. The principles of searching are the same for everyone, but vary depending on whether you are looking for a man or woman.

Searching for a man

Unlike women, men generally keep the same surname throughout their lives, which makes a search a lot easier. If you have the full name and the date of birth, and you think you know which area he lives in, you can go to a local library or on to one of the online electoral roll websites which cover the UK. If he has an unusual surname, this can often bring about a speedy conclusion to your search. If he has a common surname and there are too many people with the same name for you to contact them all, try looking under his wife's name. If you don't know her name, go back to the records and search the marriage entries to find it, then return to the electoral roll and see if you can find a listing under her name.

If you have no idea where the man is currently living, having a previous address can be helpful. You can then approach any neighbours still living in the area to see if they know where he has moved to – they might even still be in contact with him. Another option is to use local or regional newspapers, which can publish a letter from you about your search, or see if a local radio station can help. The man you are looking for might still have family or friends in that area who can point you in the right direction.

Searching for a woman

Tracing a woman can be more complicated and time-consuming, as women normally change their surnames on marriage. If you know only her maiden name and approximate date of birth, move forward eighteen to twenty years and start searching the marriage records. Work through the years until you come across her marriage entry. This will give you her husband's surname. Cross reference that in the marriage records by entering the husband's surname and the quarter of the year of marriage – e.g. April, May, June 1960 – and work down the list until you come to his surname. This entry will contain the husband's first name, as well.

Your results should look something like this:

Surname	First name	Spouse's surname	District	ref. no.
Atkins	Joanne C.	Carter	Bromsgrove	1234

The cross referenced results should look like this:

Surname	First name	Spouse's surname	District	ref. no.
Carter	Brian D.	Atkins	Bromsgrove	1234

In other words, Joanne C. Atkins and Brian D. Carter got married in Bromsgrove in the April/May/June quarter of 1960. Now go back to the electoral roll and search for a Brian D. Carter living in the same house as Joanne C. Carter. This should bring about the desired result. Of course many couples divorce and people often re-marry. So it might be necessary to repeat the procedure: i.e. starting a few years later, look through the marriage records for a remarriage (women re-marry under either their married name or maiden name, so look under both) and once you have the new husband's name, see if they are listed on the electoral roll as living at the same address.

If you have still not got a positive result, go to the births records and starting from the year of the Carter-Atkins marriage, look for any birth entries for children born of that marriage. Look through the list of Carters until you find an entry that corresponds to your search. It will look something like this:

Surname	First name	Spouse's surname	District	ref. no.
Carter	Dennis B.	Atkins	Bromsgrove	1234

Once you have discovered a birth, repeat the basic search procedure in order to trace this child, who would now be an adult. Search the electoral rolls, and in the case of a daughter, look for an entry in the marriage records to find her current surname. Once you've traced the younger-generation Carter, his/her mother shouldn't be far away.

You can order copies of the actual certificates for all the relevant entries you have discovered from the General Register Office, and these provide a lot of information and leads on which to work, such as previous addresses. It's a matter of keeping at it until you get a breakthrough. Don't give up until you have exhausted every avenue open to you.

If you have failed to trace a person using these methods, look through the deaths records to see if they have passed away. If they have, a copy of the death certificate will tell you the person's date of birth, address, where they died, cause of death and the name and address of the person who registered their death. You will at least be able to draw a line under your search.

For adoptees, the procedure for finding a birth mother is much the same. Once an adopted child (minimum age 18) obtains their original birth certificate, they have their mother's full name and address at the time of the adoption. In addition to this, an adoptee can now get their full birth record from the General Register Office. This contains much more detail: the mother's date of birth, possibly the names of her parents and any siblings she might have, as well as the address where she was living at the time of the birth. Plus additional confidential information, such as the reason the child was given up for adoption. These records are a fantastic source of information and will help greatly in finding the mother concerned through the method outlined above.

Compiled by Gill Whitley

Future developments

Earlier this year the British Library announced that it is set to digitise 40 million pages of national newspapers from the Newspaper Library at Colindale, north London, and make them available online for the first time. The process will be carried out over the next ten years. The British Library's chief executive, Dame Lynne Brindley, called it 'the most significant programme of newspaper digitisation this country has ever seen,' adding that it will 'transform a research process which previously relied on scrolling through page after page of microfilm or print.'

The new online archive will focus on specific geographic areas – and include many regional newspapers – along with selected periods such as the census years between 1841 and 1911. Other categories will focus on key events and themes, such as the Crimean War, Boer War and suffragette movement. The aim, said Dame Lynne, is to build a rich repository of easily accessible material for researchers, 'particularly in the fields of family history and genealogy'. When this ambitious programme is completed, it will provide another useful tool for anyone digging into the past to trace family members, distant relations and other contacts.

CHAPTER EIGHT

A Final Note

I want to end with a missing and found story of my own, because I think it illustrates well the slippery, unpredictable nature of the reunion process and the odd pitfalls which can lie in wait for the unsuspecting reunited.

A few years ago a childhood friend contacted me through the internet. Bobbi (not her real name) and I grew up together in New York during the sixties, which weren't very swinging for me personally. We had met at the age of ten, when our families both moved into the same suburban street, and did many of those traditional kids' activities together – we sold lemonade to passers-by from a roadside stand, we produced a neighbourhood 'newspaper', we roamed the streets together and got up to mischief. Bobbi had a slight hearing problem, but it was no big deal. I just talked louder.

We were still sort of friendly as teenagers, but had begun to grow apart. Then, straight after high school, I moved to London and began a completely new life, while Bobbi stayed behind in New York. I saw her again a few times in the mid-eighties, during my lengthy sojourn in the US. By then we were both married and I had two small sons. She said that she longed to have children, too, but her husband refused. We lost touch again after that and two more decades passed.

Then the internet worked its magic and suddenly we were e-mailing each other. Life had not been kind to Bobbi. Her hearing problem had worsened and she was now effectively deaf. The husband who had refused to have children with her had left her for another woman and – particularly cruel, this – gone on to father a child. She had fallen out with the once-close sister, who hadn't spoken to Bobbi in years. And in case all that wasn't awful enough, she'd been recently injured in a car accident and was fighting her insurance company for compensation.

Meanwhile, I'd had many blessings for which to be thankful. I had two healthy and happy sons, one of whom had recently married. I was in a stable relationship with my partner, my career was ticking over nicely and all my faculties were in order.

Naturally I was a little uncomfortable about this imbalance in our destinies. I e-mailed her warmly and encouragingly, I commiserated over her problems. I recalled our good times together, half a lifetime ago. She seemed cheerful despite her woes and I admired her upbeat attitude. Of course, it was all too apparent that we had nothing in common besides our distant, lemonade-selling past. Our e-mails didn't even seem to be written in the same language – and not just because she was wholly American and I'd been living in England most of my adult life. There seemed to be a huge cultural and social gulf between us. Still, she was a decent person, hard done by, and I felt deeply sorry for her. I was glad we were back in touch after so long.

We exchanged a few e-mails. Mine were short and snappy. Hers were long and detailed and generally full of bad news: continued battles with the insurance company, an injured arm and hand that wouldn't get better, more family disputes. The e-mails became sporadic and eventually fizzled out.

About a year later there was a major event in my world: the family's first grandchild was born. My married son and his wife had a son of their own. It was a happy time and in the days that followed I e-mailed friends around the world with the news, attaching the customary cute-sleeping-baby photo. I sent Bobbi an e-mail, too, to keep her in the loop. I expected it to elicit a reply, but I didn't receive one.

I started thinking. Had I been somehow insensitive to share my joy with her? For childless, solitary Bobbi, maybe the new baby was one blessing too far. Maybe it just served to underline how much less fortunate she was than me. Maybe she thought it callous of me to 'rub it in'.

In the end I just had to forget the whole unsettling business and move on. In any case, I told myself, it showed that the gulf between Bobbi and me was now unbridgeable. Maybe there was truth in the adage 'you can't go home again', as per the title of that old Thomas Wolfe novel. You can't recover the past.

Many months went by before I made another attempt to contact her. Once again, my e-mail went unanswered and it seemed that I had been well and truly dropped. But soon afterwards, in an idle moment and for no particular reason, I decided to Google Bobbi. She'd told me that she had got involved with a local association for deaf people, so I tapped in a few relevant words. And sure enough, her name came up.

I was stunned. It was a death notice in the *New York Times*. I looked at the date of the notice – it was about three weeks after my grandson was born.

How could she have died? I managed to find contact details for Bobbi's sister and e-mailed her. She messaged back, explaining that her car accident had left Bobbi in bad shape and due to unresolved legal wrangles over her health insurance, she didn't get the medical attention she needed. She was off work and lived alone. She got an infection and one day she just collapsed. She was found too late.

A Final Note

It's all history now, but from time to time I still wonder whether my gut feeling about Bobbi was right and she had dropped me from her life because the divide between us was too painfully clear. Or whether I'd got her completely wrong and by the time my joyful e-mail arrived announcing the baby's birth she was already too ill to respond. Perhaps she never even saw it. I'll never know.

It's difficult, perhaps impossible, truly to understand another person, whether an old friend or a new one. But it's easy to misconstrue their motives. Making contact after many years with someone from your past might be a good idea or a bad one, it might work out satisfactorily or it might not. It's usually worth a shot. But in any case, a reunion with the 'long lost' is not the ending to an old story, it's the beginning of something else.

Appendix

Websites and other resources for tracing people

For tracing family members:
www.salvationarmy.org.uk/familytracing
www.redcross.org.uk/trace
www.findaparentorchild.co.uk
www.LostCousins.com

For tracing friends:
www.friendsreunited.co.uk
www.myoldmate.net
www.lookupuk.com
www.ukpeoplefinder.com
www.lostamigos.net
www.people-search.co.uk
www.missing-you.net

For tracing old classmates:
www.classmatesreunited.co.uk
www.britainreunited.co.uk
www.ukfriendsreunited.com

For researching family trees:
www.genesreunited.co.uk
www.ancestry.co.uk
www.familyhistory.telegraph.co.uk
www.jewishgen.org

www.familytreefolk.co.uk

Genealogical researcher Roy Stockdill –roy.stockdill@btinternet.com

Family History Monthly magazine – www.familyhistorymonthly.com

Family Tree Magazine – www.family-tree.co.uk

For adoption-related searches:

www.norcap.org.uk

www.ukbirth-adoptionregister.com

www.peoplefinders.co.uk

www.julieg.f9.co.uk

Avril Ross-Wright – avril.rosswright@virgin.net

For tracing military contacts:

www.comrades-in-arms-reunited.com

www.comradesandcolleagues.com

www.forces365.com

www.britisharmedforces.org

www.forcesreunited.org.uk

www.servicepals.com

www.modreunited.co.uk

www.soldiermagazine.co.uk

www.armedforces.co.uk

www.britishlegion.org.uk

www.nationalserviceveterans association.co.uk

For tracing wartime evacuees:

www.evacuees.org.uk.

For official records of births, marriages and deaths:

www.gro.gov.uk (General Register Office)

www.nationalarchives.gov.uk
www.findmypast.co.uk
www.ancestry.co.uk
www.bmdindex.co.uk
www.ukbmd.org.uk
www.gro-scotland.gov.uk

Electoral Roll:
www.theukelectoralroll.co.uk
www.192.com/people/electoral-roll
www.tracesmart.co.uk
www.ukroll.com
www.ukphonebook.com

Private investigators:
www.theABI.org.uk (Association of British Investigators)
www.tracepeople.co.uk
www.investigationservices.co.uk

Missing people:
www.missingpeople.org.uk
www.findermonkey.co.uk